In the Event of My Untimely Demise

In the Event of
My Untimely Demise

Twenty Things My Son Needs to Know

Brian Sack

HarperOne
An Imprint of HarperCollins*Publishers*

NOTE: Names have been changed to protect the innocent or myself.

HarperCollins books may be purchased for educational, business, or sales promotional use. For information please write: Special Markets Department, HarperCollins Publishers, 10 East 53rd Street, New York, NY 10022.

HarperCollins Web site: http://www.harpercollins.com
HarperCollins®, 📖 ®, and HarperOne™ are trademarks of HarperCollins Publishers.

FIRST EDITION

Text design by Martha Blegen

Library of Congress Cataloging-in-Publication Data
Sack, Brian.
     In the event of my untimely demise / Brian Sack.
     p.   cm.
     ISBN 978–0–06–137430–2
     1. American wit and humor.   I. Title.
     PN6165.S23 2008
     814′.6–dc22   2007044767

08 09 10 11 12 RRD(H) 10 9 8 7 6 5 4 3 2 1

To Ewa

Contents

Introduction

When my mother was diagnosed with breast cancer, she was, as I remind myself every day, as old as I am now. That's to say she was not really old at all. More like advanced young. Perhaps pre-middle-aged. She was still youthful, spirited, energetic, and certainly should have had ample time here on earth to raise her three sons, sing into the cassette recorder, and eat salted tomatoes—all things she really liked to do.

Alas, it wasn't in the cards.

She hid the dim prognosis from us and fought the good fight in a four-year struggle with no shortage of peaks and valleys. Hope ebbed and flowed; there were good times, bad times, and awful times, then one day in August 1983 there was no more time at all.

But she left some instructions.

Though she'd dug in her heels at the onset of her disease and fought most valiantly, in the back of her mind she must have known she was in mortal peril. That worst-case scenario prompted her to put to paper some motherly guidance—in the event of her untimely demise.

Shortly after she succumbed—at an age I am now perilously close to myself—my father handed me an envelope. Inside were three handwritten, single-spaced pages in my mother's trademark fancy cursive. Whoever taught her cursive did a great job; meanwhile mine looks like Arabic written while fleeing a mob.

When I read my mother's letter, I could hear her voice as she lamented the prospect of her death and hoped her children would make the most of the future without her.

Many times when we're referring to the desires of deceased relatives, we say, "Arthur would have wanted this . . ." or "Tilly would never have approved . . ." but I'm lucky. I don't have to guess. What I should or shouldn't be doing is likely to be found somewhere in those few pages.

"Don't do anything foolish with your life," was an understandable motherly plea. Though I've certainly done many foolish things, thanks to her I made sure not to wager my entire life on them in almost all instances.

Admittedly I did not fully honor her request to avoid "taking foolish risks with drugs + alcohol + automobiles"—after all, I went to college—but I can say that I didn't take *overly* foolish risks during my immortal twenties.

That letter became and remains a priceless connection to her. In fact, it's the only connection to her aside from a hand-knit pink cardigan I'm not about to wear anytime soon.

I kept the letter in a safe place and even made backup copies in case there was a fire or a glacier melted. Every so often I'd take it out and consult it. Sometimes to console myself with words from the mother I missed dearly. Other times to try to seduce a girl by showing her my emotional side. If you believe that to be in poor taste, let me remind you that on page 2, Mother specifically states, "Find someone to love you and who you love."

I did, though it took a while.

When the someone I loved—my wife, Ewa—announced she was pregnant, I realized I, too, would have a child in need of parental guidance—in the event of my untimely demise.

Ecstatic with the news, I started writing a book specifically for our as-yet unborn child. The working title was understandably *For My As-Yet Unborn Child*. It was a collection of lighthearted, tongue-in-cheek essays for the aforementioned child-to-be. But when Ewa had a miscarriage, my motivation and sense of humor were temporarily immobilized, and I stopped writing the book.

When Ewa became pregnant the second time, I was ecstatic again. I immediately resumed the book. It was still a collection of lighthearted, tongue-in-cheek essays. It was still for our as-yet unnamed child, albeit a different one. But when she had a second miscarriage, my motivation and sense of humor were again temporarily immobilized, and again I stopped writing the book.

When Ewa became pregnant the third time, I was less ecstatic. I'd say I was more cautiously optimistic, as you'd be if a pretty girl said she liked your pink cardigan, or you heard through the grapevine that you might be getting a promotion. I was not about to assume anything might pan out. I was also certain of a supernatural book-miscarriage connection. As a result, I did not resume writing the book, which would have been a collection of lighthearted, tongue-in-cheek essays for our as-yet unborn child.

Except for Ewa and me having totally incompatible blood, the pregnancy was nearly flawless. Thanks to modern science, our plasma reconciled, and nine months later—right on target—Ewa gave birth to an awesome and wonderful baby boy.

The experience took my breath away, though I had enough left to repeatedly exclaim, "Oh my God!" as Dr. Baxi relentlessly peppered me with questions about the pediatrician I'd forgotten to line up.

We had a son. He had no pediatrician lined up. But even worse: *He had no book.*

Until now.

Brian Sack

NEW YORK CITY

Dear Son:

Nondairy creamer is flammable, and your marriage will suffer if you go skinny-dipping with cheerleaders.

That's knowledge and wisdom, respectively.

Having things like that in our brains is what sets us apart from ostriches and carp. We're smarter. We think. We know things.

What does a dog think when he hears a ridiculously loud motorcycle? Bark, bark, bark. But a human is different. Humans process things. They think, That guy is trying to compensate for something.

See? We're smarter.

It's no coincidence that pigs can't drive. A ferret has never been president. Not a single llama has ever walked on the moon. Even the mighty lion with his limb-crushing teeth and bowel-curdling roar is helpless versus a camouflaged Gary Coleman with a sniper rifle. We are the kings of the animal kingdom.

Hooray for us. We're great. But should we just rest on our laurels and be happy that we can outfox a chimp? Nein, I say. And I'm not even German. That's how strongly I feel.

Simply by virtue of being born human, we've automatically matriculated into Great Big University—a school with a staggering curriculum and a campus that stretches as far as the eye can see. The problem is, they have the worst admissions policy ever. Absolutely everyone gets in. There's not even a bar to raise or lower. So, sure, enrollment means you're smarter than a chimp—but by how much?

I want to help.

As a dad, I want my child to be the best, the smartest, the greatest. This book is my earnest attempt to help you achieve all those superlatives—my effort to give you a leg up at Great Big University. Assuming you can read, you'll have access to some of the knowledge and wisdom I've picked up over the years. The things that left impressions, taught me lessons, made me a better student—not in the school sense, because technically I was a lousy student, but in the life sense.

These are the things I think you should know, the things I want you to know. The things I hope will set you apart from all the riffraff at Great Big University. It is automatic insight that quite possibly may come in handy sometime. Faced with a situation or dilemma, you'll be able to say, "You know—Dad told me about this. And I'd know what to do had I not skimmed that particular chapter."

So don't skim.

Think of this book as a CliffsNotes of some sort— but instead of learning who poisoned whom at the end of Hamlet, you're learning about Frenchmen, parenthood, marriage, and some middle-school terrorist who kept standing on my toe.

I truly hope this book is just the beginning of a lifelong quest to obtain and retain knowledge and wisdom. You can never have too much of that. The more of it you possess, the farther you'll find yourself from something that pecks, slithers, hisses, or throws poo.

And that, darling son, is a good thing.

Love,
Your Father

Children laugh about
four hundred times a day,
while adults laugh on average
only fifteen times a day.
That's because children
don't have to change diapers
or run from subpoenas.

1

Change Starts at Conception

To preserve yourself as the center of the world, to stay
your own best authority on everything, your own expert on
all topics, infallible, omniscient. Always, every time of the
month, forever: Use birth control.

Chuck Palahniuk

Any dad will tell you the birth of their first child is one of the
most incredible, momentous events of their lives. It's an un-
forgettable milestone, not only because it signifies his tran-
sition into fatherhood, but because he sees a tiny shrieking
head coming out of his wife's vagina.

Until that defining moment, a father-to-be has spent
nine months hearing from everyone who has ever had a
child. New parents, old parents, it doesn't matter. The fact
that they have already entered the realm of parenthood enti-
tles them, obligates them, to share their little secret. It goes
pretty much, actually exactly, like this:

"First kid?"

"Yup."

"Things are going to change."

So, take it from me, another parent with a secret to share:

things are going to change. Hopefully you will have already been aware of this.

It should not be news to an expecting parent that a baby is at the very least a major lifestyle disruption. It's one of only a few occasions, such as a first wedding or domicile relocation, that warrant a mass announcement. Even photo cards. It's an event so momentous it qualifies you for tax breaks. It gives you the right to unapologetically miss work. It is, in most every way, an extremely important event followed by approximately eighteen years of other, not insignificant, events. It is the beginning of an amazing adventure; like Homer's *Odyssey*, but with less sailing.

You should certainly be well aware of this by the pregnancy's third trimester—in layman's terms, the time right before all hell breaks loose. By this time, your wife has a studio apartment where her stomach was. Even being tired exhausts her. If watching your waddling, uncomfortable, ragged wife moan down the hallway doesn't suggest even vaguely that your life is going to change, you probably shouldn't be having a baby. The cruel irony, of course, being that by then it's far too late to have reached that conclusion.

However, you can be forgiven for not having the slightest clue as to how your life will change. That particular wisdom only comes from experience, from baptism by fire.

Though I will endeavor to shed some light on what one can expect with the creation and introduction of a dependent life form, please be aware that the reality of parenthood is terribly difficult to express, and I can't truly do it justice.

It does not lend itself easily to words, nor can it be better explained through songs and gesticulating. Like weightlessness and Tommy Lee driving a boat with an erection, parenting is something that demands it be experienced firsthand to be fully appreciated. Trying to explain parenthood to a nonparent is like trying to explain the sun to a drunken hillbilly. Sure, they'll nod and smile and stagger away with the basics—big and hot—but they won't really grasp the sheer magnitude.

To force an analogy that needlessly incorporates Australia: Parenting is like emigrating to Australia in the 1800s. A person heard about it through word of mouth and written accounts and was vaguely aware of an exciting, interesting, and challenging new environment. But he wouldn't think much of it until one day he found himself headed there. After a long, tiresome journey, he'd arrive, and only then realize that he had absolutely no idea what he was getting himself into. The animals bounce, the seasons are backward, and everyone around him speaks the same language but uses totally different words. And there's really no going back because it was a one-way trip.

Nevertheless, I feel it's important you have some perspective on the changes brought by parenthood and how something that does nothing but soil itself and weep at odd hours can have such an absolutely staggering impact on your life.

There are many roads to having a baby, especially in this day and age, but to facilitate matters we'll stick with the traditional one: You find someone you want to marry, they feel the same way, and sooner or later you decide to have a baby. You will then do your thing, with the knowledge that if you are successful, you will wind up adding a baby to the equation—thus changing your life in some fashion. There are no major changes yet, aside from the meticulous planning of coitus—because at that point you're merely trying to have a baby. That endeavor can range from a laborious undertaking to, in my case, a terrifyingly effortless three minutes. But there is no actual baby. It remains a distant notion. Just as a bepimpled pubescent teen imagines how one day he'll lose his virginity, a maturing man imagines how he'll one day become a father. But losing one's virginity seldom comes to pass as one had imagined. The fantasy is a swollen-lipped, airbrushed Playmate swimming in satin sheets. The reality is your bum on cold vinyl and Maggie whacking her head on the rearview mirror as she steals your innocence in the passenger seat of a Scirocco; your rapid heartbeat the result not of passion, but terror that every passing vehicle's headlights will somehow illuminate you through the frosted windows.

In that same manner, becoming a parent is also something you can't possibly fathom—like being attacked by an enraged neon monkey in a top hat.

Though subtle, change starts at conception. Your wife, having peed on an expensive plastic stick, emerges from the bathroom with an expression of glee, one hopes, and waves the stick in your face. You consult the box it came in to make sure you're reading the stick correctly. If you have, congratulations are in order. Still, there are variables. The pregnancy could fail. And anyway, the real change is nine months away. Nine months is nearly a year, and a year seems like forever. Granted, the older you get, the less like forever it seems—but it's still significantly down the road. The only immediate change this early into the game is that mom-to-be cannot continue drinking and smoking like she used to. If she didn't know that, she probably shouldn't be having a baby, either.

Eventually the pregnancy begins to show, and you realize that, yes, things will change—but it's still a fairly abstract idea. The only real change you see is in your wife and her hormonal fluctuations. She loves you, she hates you, she loves you, she hates you. One moment she's moon-bat crazy for steak; the next it's strawberries, feta cheese, Ben & Jerry's, tomatoes. During the infancy of the pregnancy, you notice strangers hesitating as they quietly try to determine if your wife is pregnant or just out of shape.

And then there's a little more change. Old boyfriends—the ones who've made brief appearances during the course of your relationship—hear the news, dashing any hopes they may have had against the rocks. They force a smile, wish you luck, and quietly withdraw from your lives, any torch they may have held having been extinguished by the news.

As time passes, your wife looks like she's smuggling a softball, then a football, and then a basketball. It becomes more and more apparent that something's going on. You come to realize that inside your beloved is a restless little creature—one you helped make. It kicks and punches, turns and hiccups. It uses your wife's bladder as a pillow, sending her to the bathroom every five minutes. You realize change is coming, but it still only manifests itself as an anonymous entity in sonograms with clarity as elusive as the Loch Ness Monster.

But life still proceeds fairly normally, and aside from a bloated, miserable spouse dashing to the bathroom when she's not raiding the fridge for salmon or cupcakes, there's little to suggest the real drama that awaits. You can still see movies when you want and sleep in when you can. You can be spontaneous, unless it involves your wife jogging. Any real change is self-imposed: the more neurotic among us panicking about room decor—as if an infant cares about wall treatments. We hold baby showers and move furniture around. We familiarize ourselves with the nomenclature of new parents: words like *onesie*, *Bugaboo*, and *swaddle*. We shop for cribs and clothes and take informed positions on issues we hadn't ever cared about, like the pros and cons of circumcision, and breast-feeding versus formula.

In the final weeks before the due date, the reality of sweeping lifestyle reform finally begins to sink in. As the days tick away, the change is tangible. You can now imagine, in some small way, the potential impact this third party could have on your evenings out. On your work. On your spare time. On your life in general and your future as a whole.

And then come the lasts. The last time you'll sleep in on a Sunday. The last time you can dash out to meet your friends for happy hour. The last time you can leave windows open or pennies on the floor. You're days away from a new level of anxiety in air travel. A world of standing in the kitchen half-conscious, warming milk. A time when the freedom provided during your child's naptime is so precious that anything that could disturb it—a phone call, a knock on the door, a dog's bark—can leave you cringing and cursing. Soon there'll be a time when your time is no longer your time.

Regret sets in. Maybe you should have traveled more. Spent more time as a married couple. Had more sex. Lived abroad. Made more money. You're on the cusp of something big, a major change. Even so, it's something you still fail to fully understand—like the appeal of poker.

And then, D-day. Though you've had nine months to dig in and prepare for the invasion, you're not really ready. The armada is on the horizon. As you race to the hospital, it occurs to you that the life you've had will very shortly cease to be. You'll enter a couple, leave a family.

In the delivery room your wife curses you for doing this to her. She barks at you for ice, you bastard. And she feels the pain associated with the equivalent of pooping a watermelon. I can tell you now, this is the worst time to suggest she forego the epidural. I strongly recommend you obey the first and pretty much only rule of your wife in labor: Shut up and do exactly what she says.

Despite the fact you're witnessing one of life's most natural events, there's little natural about it. Show me a guy who's used to a crowd of strangers staring at his wife's crotch and cheering her on, and I'll show you a guy who's married to a stripper in Tijuana.

And your poor wife's private parts. Armageddon. Territory you'd once treated like your own personal Disney World now resembles a New Jersey industrial disaster. There's your poor old buddy—bruised, battered, and bloodied like she went ten rounds with Tyson. All you can do is look on helplessly and encourage her to "push" as she screams and huffs and puffs and digs her fingers into your arm like it was fresh Play Doh.

And then, with a final push, your child is born. From the chaos and gore, a baby—your baby—and as it coughs and sputters and shrieks, the reality hits you. It's magical, surreal, amazing: the universally understood moment that every parent talks about. The instant when you realize life is forever different no matter what happens. The center of your universe is relocated. What was so important mere minutes ago is laughably insignificant now. Life is no longer all about you; it's all about *that*. And *that* is the soggy, wrinkled, shocked little creature now resting on your wife's empty belly. Behold, your greatest creation and your greatest Achilles' heel. There's no going back. Though you can be an ex-husband, a lapsed Catholic, a former heavyweight, or a deposed king—you will always be a father. It's one title that can never, ever be taken away from you.

From this point onward, your heart now resides outside of you, remanded to the custody of something wholly incapable of taking care of itself. Something seemingly bent on its own self-destruction. The coming years of your life will now be suicide watch, a twenty-four-hour job centered around this selfish little creature who cries and screams, keeps you up, slows you down, and poops as soon as you dress it. A priceless Fabergé egg with legs. A tiny little thing that is utterly powerless, yet has the ability to enrich your life as you've never imagined or to turn it completely upside down with no notice at all.

Finally, this momentous, terrifying, incredible moment makes it all clear. You realize that your decision of little over nine months ago—as minor as it may have seemed at the time—was the greatest and most significant decision you've ever made in your life. As your exhausted wife drifts off to sleep and you stare at the amazing creature you both created, it finally hits you: *Things really are going to change.*

Elvis Presley got a C in his eighth-grade music class, yet became a music legend. But he also died on the toilet. So, maybe we shouldn't celebrate mediocre grades after all.

2

High, Reasonable Hopes

All you need in this life is ignorance and confidence;
then success is sure.

Mark Twain

I grew up in what I understood to be a meritocracy, a system wherein the folks who worked the hardest and excelled the most could expect to reap benefits exceeding those of the average person. It was reasonable to assume that Joanna—who read her books and did the homework she was assigned—would enter a better academic institution than Todd—who smoked pot and watched TV all day. You'd have been hard-pressed to find someone who would argue that Todd's memorization of every *Star Trek* plot point placed him on an equal footing with Joanna when it came to admission to Harvard. Indeed, last I heard, Joanna had her Ivy League sheepskin while Todd was fermenting mushroom juice with a bisexual Wiccan he met in a forest party.

As a young advertising-agency writer, it made sense that I would make more money than my unemployed roommate because I got up at 7 a.m. and went to work, while he got up at 4 p.m. and went to sofa. I don't think he'd disagree that our salary inequality was logical and pretty fair, seeing as he was always well rested.

When we look at the biographies of the mega-accomplished among us (actually, they live away from us because they can afford to), there is an undeniable pattern that emerges. Their histories are almost interchangeable: At fifteen Mr. X started working in the such-and-such industry. He left the army and was accepted to Yale, which he paid for himself by working two full-time jobs. He graduated magna cum laude and opened his own business sixteen minutes after the commencement speech ended.

Even when these guys drop out of college, it's because they were too busy overachieving to bother with school. Bill Gates is a dropout. Seems to be doing okay. Guys like Bill have something most of us haven't got, and it's not just billions and billions of dollars. It's a determination, talent, and intellect that lies dormant in most folks. By "dormant" I mean there's a good chance it's not there.

I not only expect those people to be better off than I, but I want them to be. That's because of my belief in the meritocracy. Their accomplishment sends a message, and the message is: *If you lie stoned on the sofa all day, no Lexus for you.* I think that's a good message.

When my friend John would excuse himself early on weekend evenings to go home and practice his guitar, I understood that this sacrifice of his made him more likely than me to become a rock star—especially since I quit after my first piano lesson and spent two years sitting in the back of band class faking the trumpet. So devoted was John to his hoped-for musical career that nothing could separate him from his daily guitar practicing—not ladies we'd met, not my pleas to stay out a little later, nothing. When the mood to practice hit him, as it often did, he was on his way home with no reservations. I admired his determination and was certain that his sacrifices would one day pay off. And they did. His amazing talents with a guitar ultimately helped him become a rock star, just like he'd imagined would happen. I had no problem with this. Although I have a musical sense and could probably craft some clever lyrics, this was not a slot I had any logical hope of filling. Now he sleeps with supermodels and has many millions more dollars than I can probably hope to earn. All well deserved, of course. Another tale for the meritocracy files.

Alas, at some point in my lifetime and prior to yours, the system changed. Now we no longer live in a meritocracy as much as we do a wantocracy—wherein a tone-deaf person with no musical training or skill thinks it's perfectly normal to expect to be the next David Bowie—because he'd really like that to happen. My point is made every season on *American Idol* when we watch some of the nation's least talented individuals aspire to fill positions that not too long ago would have been considered outrageously unachievable. How a heavily bruised four-hundred-pound girl with a Marlboro-tainted larynx can think the world is hankering to hear her forget someone else's lyrics is beyond me—but not beyond the countless individuals who, like Enorma McCantsing, express shock and dismay to discover in front of thirty-eight million people that screeching and stumbling through a Britney cover has only enriched our lives, not theirs.

We live in a generation in which some people mistake wanting something for deserving it and in which the bar for what some consider talent is so low that not even the limbo community's most elite could pass under it.

I don't want you to be that person who puts himself out there to have dreams he should never have had in the first place dashed in a grand spectacle before a commercial break. I don't want my child's hubris and/or naïveté winding up in a YouTube clip to accidentally entertain the masses. For your benefit, and mine, I offer you this sage advice:

Have high, reasonable hopes.

These four words will save you—and your relatives—a lot of grief and embarrassment. It should seem like common sense, but common sense is like a Rubik's Cube: we recall having it for a while but don't exactly remember what we did with it.

I have met people who neither finished college nor held a job, yet spend their time imagining themselves as CEO of an as-yet-unnamed megacorporation. I know untrained, untalented actors with awful fake accents who expect to be film stars someday. Some of the least funny people I've ever met were in a comedy class—certain they would eventually entertain a large audience that did not consist entirely of sympathetic, tortured family members.

While some of these people are completely lazy and un-motivated, others are very driven—taking lessons, perform-ing, generating endless screenplays and business plans—unfortunately they're just not good at it. Regardless of their energy level, all these individuals share one quality that I hope you will not develop and that I will try my hardest not to impart to you: complete and utter self-delusion.

I want you to have big, reasonable dreams. I want you to succeed. I'm not saying, "You can't"; I'm just saying, "Don't fool yourself if you can't."

As clichéd as it may sound, anything is possible. History is filled with people of all types and backgrounds who, espe-cially in a country like the United States, have been able to cut amazing paths for themselves. You *can* be an astronaut, or a president, or a movie star, or a guy who makes crossword puzzles I can't finish. But it's important that you realize there are ways of getting there—and they're seldom easy.

Wanting to be something is the first step, not the final step—a common mistake many people make before ap-pearing on Fox to be eviscerated by Simon Cowell. The big mistake that people make is forgetting that wanting to be something has to be followed up with action to make that happen, coupled with the ability to be self-critical and rea-sonable. If you can be honest with yourself—sooner than later—it will prevent you from finding yourself onstage at forty-three in a dingy nightclub with an audience of eight people watching your soul die.

So, you *can* do it. Dream big, practical dreams. Have high, reasonable hopes.

This epidemic of overly confident, incredibly nontalented individuals with unrealistic expectations can be explained as the unfortunate by-product of a few things. The first of which, I believe, was the epidemic of political correctness that started in the eighties. PC began with the best of intentions, but, like a bad rehearsal-dinner speech from a mean-spirited best man, got ugly and uncomfortable. It created a culture—a not very bright one—that was passionate about not wanting to hurt anyone's feelings. With its simplistic logic, calling someone "African American" rather than "black" took care of decades of inequality. Calling a handicapped child someone with "special needs" would eliminate the challenges of having a handicapped child. Your busboy went from "illegal" to "undocumented"—even though in reality he could be deported either way. Everyone believed things could be fixed with words.

This linguistic claptrap became a BBM (Big, Beautiful Monster) with gigantic, intellectually challenged tentacles that reached out and strangled other aspects of our lives. Suddenly teachers didn't grade in red ink because it was "hurtful," and teams no longer competed for points because that might imply one team was actually better than the other. Everyone got ribbons just for showing up at the race, lest they feel excluded. According to the profiles on Match.com, we're all "very good-looking," too.

It's no wonder, then, that the end result is a generation or two of people who've never heard a discouraging word; people for whom the suggestion that they can't direct, paint, sing, or make flan is incomprehensible.

Now, take those same folks and put them in today's dual-income society, with Mom and Dad feeling guilty for not spending as much time with their children as they'd like. The moment the nanny goes home, the guilty parents fire up the coddling: *Everything you do is great! You're the best! G'night!*

The consequence of this—as we see on TV far too often—is a kid who has spent a childhood being praised for merely existing. A child who never failed because failure was unpossible. A child who thinks *unpossible* is a word. Family, friends, and society never once critiqued his abilities because under the laws of political correctness, constructive criticism became hate speech.

And so, we're left with a child who dreams so big and stupid he spends two days sleeping in a tent for the chance to butcher "Proud Mary" in front of his countrymen. Great entertainment, indeed, but I don't want that to be you.

Oftentimes a spouse in
the beginning stages of
an affair will be unusually
attentive. The next time
your significant other seems
overly pleasant, accuse her
of infidelity and set the
record straight.

3

Trust Your Gut

Trust your instinct to the end,
though you can render no reason.

Ralph Waldo Emerson

The human being is the only animal in the kingdom that will actively overrule basic instinct. When our gut tells us not to enter the elevator because there's a scary man in it, we tell our gut to be quiet because we don't want to hurt the scary man's feelings by bolting. So we enter the elevator, and moments later as we're being knifed in the belly by the scary man, we realize we should have trusted our instinct in the first place.

The rest of the animal kingdom has no problem acknowledging what their gut tells them and acting upon it posthaste. They make no attempt to rationalize or overthink their subconscious analysis. They don't care about hurting your feelings or if their actions seem illogical, offensive, politically incorrect, or insane. They won't tell themselves things like, *Oh, don't be silly.* If their gut says, *Run!* that's exactly what they'll do.

We, too, come equipped with a highly evolved early-warning system that manages to pick up things that aren't necessarily visible on the surface. It's like Gaydar, but for danger. It makes immediate assessments of people and environments and dictates a course of action: Don't get in that car. Do not go into the dark stairwell. Avoid striking up a conversation with that woman.

Our nerves are there to keep us alive, to alert us to the fact there's a problem and we're causing harm to our bodies. Without nerves we'd keep burning our hand on the stove, not know we were being stabbed in the back, and not realize we'd broken our arm when we fell off the ladder. Without nerves, it's safe to say most of us would be dead in record time.

Our instinct is there to keep us away from dangerous situations and out of harm's way. It lets us know when something's not quite right, when someone is not quite right. It's our own personal Paul Revere. I don't know the exact workings of it, of course, but it explains why some people rub you the wrong way before they've said two words, and why certain situations give you a vague sense of discomfort. Not *Star Trek* convention discomfort, but that eerie feeling you get when someone is approaching you. The sense that something's not right, even though you can't quite put your finger on it.

I remember quite clearly the sense of impending danger I felt one night many years ago while playing darts in a bar.

I felt very distracted and couldn't relax, even with the assistance of my friend, beer. My gut said to leave. Eventually I listened and headed for the door—just as a brawl broke out. We can perceive much more than we give ourselves credit for. How we act on that information, however, is completely up to us.

With a tip of the hat to the dolphin community, we humans are technically the smartest things on the planet. Unfortunately with that intelligence comes the very bad habit of dulling our subconscious sense. Our gut tells us one thing, but our brain asks for a second opinion, challenges the original assessment, and tries to rationalize. *Bob wouldn't do that; he goes to church every Sunday. It can't be Bob.* And when it turns out it was Bob all along, we often find ourselves saying, *You know, I kind of had a feeling it was Bob.*

If your gut could say, "I told you so," it would be saying, "I told you so" a great deal. But your gut can't speak. It's like a mime waving frantically at you, desperately trying to get your attention.

My friend Dave is a perfect example of someone who has managed to completely stifle and overrule his animal instinct. Nature has developed this instinct over thousands and thousands of years, saving our ancestors from wooly mammoths and ill-tempered Neanderthals, yet Dave has all but smothered his Spidey Sense with pillows.

Dave is lucky in that he's charming and likable. People take to him immediately, offering him lucrative jobs, friendship, drinks. He often finds himself on VIP lists for no apparent reason. Doormen welcome him into their clubs while thirty other people in line wonder who the hell he is. People like Dave. Lots of people like Dave. And many of them are scary. Unfortunately, Dave does not actively consult with his gut when making decisions. For that reason, there is nothing you could say or do that would keep Dave from inviting you to be his roommate. As a result, through Dave I have met numerous individuals who have set off alarms and raised flags. People whose auras scream *beware*. The energy they emit, negative. Their very essence a combination of adjectives like *shady, dangerous, discomforting, untrustworthy, awkward*, and *peculiar*.

When Dave introduced me to Antonio, I didn't like Antonio. I couldn't say why, but I didn't want to spend time with Dave and Antonio. Unfortunately, the combination of me being Dave's friend, me having few friends, and me liking to go out meant I had to spend time with Antonio. Dave may have been oblivious, but the brief time I did spend with Antonio had my inner mime going absolutely ballistic. Practically everything Antonio did and said warranted a red flag. Antonio lived in a posh apartment and drove a phenomenally expensive car, yet never seemed to be working. He told us he imported vitamins. Yet he told others he was a screenwriter. And others he was a producer. And others a musician. He had an apartment in Miami. And he was a hotelier, he said. Of course, he didn't seem to know anything about the hotel business, but who's asking? He claimed to have a busy social schedule, yet he was always available. Once he pointed to a gorgeous girl he was with and suggested she was "the one." Later he told us she was a high-class prostitute. Like a really bad witness, Antonio's stories changed every time he told them.

He seemed incapable of being honest and most certainly was hiding things from us. Was he an insecure drug dealer? No idea. Spoiled trust-funder who'd lost his way? No idea. *Run, Dave,* I would tell Dave.

Antonio called a lot and got very upset when Dave didn't return the call right away. "He called me eight times today," Dave would complain. *Run, Dave,* I would say.

Eventually Dave listened to my instinct and actually ran. By ran I mean he stopped returning Antonio's calls. Although we honestly have no idea, we decided Antonio was a disturbed, yet rich individual who lived in a fantasy world and needed friends badly. All of this could have been avoided if Dave had trusted my gut, or even his own.

Of course, Dave wasted no time in befriending Giyal, an illegal alien with a drug problem who was prone to asking strangers if he could use their shower. *Run, Dave,* I said.

Instinct is like a muscle; it needs to be exercised. Ignore it, and you run the risk of it atrophying. That's when you find yourself saying, *I should have seen this coming,* or *I can't believe I'm being whacked.* With practice, you will be able to discern the legitimate warnings from the false alarms. Your skills improve with practice. Take wine, for example. At first, wine just tastes like wine, but the more you drink, the better you become at detecting subtle hints of caramel and spice.

I've made my own mistakes, ignored warning signs and my better judgment for a variety of reasons.

Gerry was Irish, a condition that led me to forgive his dark demeanor and uncultured behavior. Although we spent a lot of time together, mostly in bars, I could never fully let my guard down with him. Had he not had a thick brogue from the wrong side of Dublin, he'd probably not have been someone I'd share space with. He bragged he'd spent time in an English prison for assisting the IRA in a bank robbery. He liked to get drunk, make trouble, and include me in on it. One late night, I found myself frantically fleeing a police officer he'd threatened from the comfort of my vehicle. This is not a situation I'd get into on my own. Believe me when I say the sound of a police baton striking your car is unpleasant, as were the several days spent wondering if the officer had managed to memorize my license plate as he ran screaming down the street after us. Fortunately, he wasn't a multitasker, and a week later I worked up the nerve to take my car out of the garage.

With friends like Gerry, you need good lawyers.

Though I was often tempted to detach myself from Gerry, he had moments when he'd redeem himself, or perhaps not redeem himself so much as make someone *else* feel uncomfortable. He happily collected money that was owed me by a deadbeat roommate, and as a sidekick when we went out had the deterring effect of a Doberman. He attracted a certain kind of woman, but repelled the kind I liked. I wasn't scared of Gerry, just wary, but I knew I'd made a mistake in making his acquaintance. You might befriend a tiger, but as Siegfried's friend Roy learned, it's a tiger. Fortunately he spared me any significant decision making by joining the army to earn American citizenship. That gave me the opportunity to break free. Before shipping out, he claimed he had a check coming and asked if he could borrow $100 until it arrived. I knew he was lying and would disappear with the money, but I also knew that for $100 I could buy my way out of the mistake I'd made when I told my instinct to shut up.

A properly honed instinct works for more than just evaluating people. When I was offered a job with an advertising agency, my gut said, *Run, Brian*. The money wasn't bad, but it was a mediocre agency with mediocre clients, and the president obsessed with his hair to the point of absurdity. Rumor had it that while on a business trip, he'd refused to leave his hotel room until the vice president brought him some hair spray. The creative director aspired to do good work, but there was no indication we could do good work because the president's main interest was satisfying his clients. For a creative type, that seldom translates to a rewarding portfolio of work.

I knew I'd made a big mistake the moment I said yes and took the job. My disenchantment grew exponentially. Within seven weeks my boss—whom I'd describe as nonconfrontational—fired me by leaving a note on my chair. After that I told you so, I decided to pay more attention to the little mime inside me.

And so should you. Don't be afraid to trust your gut; it's more reliable than you'd think. Though we may have outgrown our use for the appendix, we'll always have a need for the natural ability to determine when we're in danger of bodily harm, bad acquaintance, or doomed employment.

And even if your gut leads you astray every now and then, making a few faulty assessments over time beats getting on the wrong elevator even once.

It takes someone
from 3 to 90 seconds
to form opinions of an
individual, according
to some big jerk
I overheard.

Bullies often come from homes with little emotional support, detached parenting, or abusive parents. The next time you get bullied, ask the aggressor if he has an unhappy home life. If he says yes, you'll know why he's making you drink from the toilet.

4

Fight, Cub

Show me a man who has enjoyed his school days,
and I'll show you a bully and a bore.

Robert Morely

I would like for you to thoroughly understand the importance of self-defense. Being able to stand up for oneself, one's friends, and one's family is crucial. I say this with the total acknowledgment that I've made a mockery of the concept—standing up for things I should have sat down for, turning cheeks when I should have swung at them, and accidentally hitting one of my few friends in the head with a rock when I should have not been hitting one of my few friends in the head with a rock. Nevertheless, the decisions I have made—bad and good as they were—all taught me something. The end result is that I possess wisdom on the subject of self-defense. I know what works, what doesn't work, and what happens when you hit Dan in the head with a rock when trying to save him.

Armed with what I know, the memories of conflicts engaged in and avoided, battles won and lost, I can hopefully help you understand when self-defense is warranted or demanded, when diplomacy is called for, and when you should simply run away like a frightened, shrieking teen.

Let it be said that fighting is barbaric and witless, and there are seldom times when it is truly warranted. The fact that in this twenty-first century we're still clubbing one another over the head for a variety of reasons suggests some sort of grand societal failure. Sure, we have tuxedos and aftershave, but in the end there's little to separate us from warring monkeys. We've been to the moon, cured heinous diseases, invented opera, yet there are still countless individuals who would uppercut you for vocalizing your dislike of the Red Sox.

In this day and age, we should be settling conflicts without violence—physical interaction being the nuclear option in any encounter. Barring home invasion and unprovoked assault, one hopes most quarrels can be worked out through diplomacy, or less nobly through sprinting. I've never truly understood the ease with which some individuals resort to brutality—how a glance taken the wrong way escalates to fisticuffs; how a stupid comment results in a black eye; why chatting up someone else's girlfriend can escalate to a molar embedded in the knuckle.

I'm not a fighter. Never was and never wanted to be. As someone who was gangly, awkward, and shy, I wasn't built for it. And as someone who liked to feel smart, fighting felt like failure; a step backward for humankind. That uncomfortable song and dance with the clichéd threats, the sleeves rolling up, the pushing and punching—very tiresome and very silly. Fighting was the pastime of those I had no interest in knowing or being like. People I didn't want a piece of. I never understood the urge to pick on someone, to threaten him because of the way he walked or the pants he wore. Perhaps that comes from the fact I walked with my shoulders hunched over and wore Sears Toughskins.

As you get older, the opportunities for getting into fights will be fewer and farther between. Unless you live in Boston. Nowhere else in the country have I found such a hair-trigger male populace so ready to throw down over a glance. So, if you find yourself about to get bopped in the nose for no apparent reason, my guess is you're either near the Big Dig or in the Big House. You can move from Boston, but if you're in prison, you'll just have to beat everyone else up. That's how you survive there, so I've heard.

Throughout my life I've been able to settle the bulk of my conflicts through diplomacy, or in some cases total cowardice. Seldom have I resorted to striking or strangling.

When the threat of conflict exists, an immediate assessment of the situation is called for. You have to size up your potential foe, evaluate the problem, determine the merits of victory or retreat, and realize how important its outcome is to you. Is conflict inevitable? Is this an issue worth standing up for? Am I about to split Dan's skull open with a rock? These are some of the questions you should be asking yourself.

My experience is limited, thankfully, but there have been occasions. Of those I will share with you the more memorable ones—and what lessons I believe you can take from them.

Simon, the Daily Annoyance

Assuming he wasn't out sick, Simon spent an entire year of middle-school homeroom stepping on my toes and asking me if his doing so was painful. Eager not to capitulate and give Simon the satisfaction of knowing he was, in fact, killing my toes, I would deny feeling any pain. This, of course, was an outright lie: Having an eighth-grader standing on my toes did hurt. My denial would inevitably cause Simon to apply more pressure to my toes, thus delivering more pain, which I would again deny feeling. It was a vicious cycle that was only interrupted by the Pledge of Allegiance. This happened most every day for a solid year in middle school, enough that I still retain a tremendous dislike for Simon, even after all these years. In fact, it's all I really remember about middle school, aside from the time I stapled my fingernail in front of an indifferent teacher.

My intention to deny Simon the pleasure of hurting me could be construed as clever—after all, he wanted a reaction, and I wouldn't give it to him. I was smarter than Simon, and in that sense I won the battle. But the fact I let this continue for practically every homeroom could be construed as me being a milquetoast. Ultimately, I lost the war.

Anything gained by my Ghandi-esque cheek turning was pointless because it resulted in me starting every day with feelings of helplessness, regret, and notably sore toes. In this case, self-defense was warranted. At the very least, a firm cease and desist should have been issued—though a punch to the crotch would have been more satisfying and most likely ended things once and for all. I hope that if you find yourself in a similar predicament, you will realize that any pain resulting from an ensuing one-time fight certainly outweighs the pain of having your toes crushed on a regular basis.

Giganto, the Psychotic Wonder Freak

Giganto was well known on the high-school grounds as being a complete and utter mental case. God knows what his glandular issues were, but the freshman monster dwarfed most, if not all, upperclassmen. In addition to being physically imposing, he was armed with the brain wattage of a polyp and the demeanor of a tortured pit bull. With a giant, ill-tempered psychotic meandering about between classes, it was only a matter of time before one crossed paths with him, and as he was perpetually scowling and poised to attack, this was never a good thing.

When my time came to be set upon, I'd foolishly asked for it. I had been emboldened by the fact he'd not yet attacked me, choosing instead to inflict his torture on others. But that had nothing to do with him not wanting to attack me and everything to do with the fact I spent a lot of time in a darkened computer room or sitting alone in the theater alcove during lunch. This somehow led me to believe I was safe.

One weekend night, while out with what friends I had, I'd heard there was a party. The party, unfortunately, was being thrown by one of Giganto's siblings, and by default was at Giganto's house. Though this was a potentially terrifying prospect, the fact that Giganto had other more stable siblings allayed my fears. And so, encouraged by my two fun-seeking passengers, we went. Just three bored high-school guys looking for something to do.

The moment Giganto answered the door, I realized I'd made a terrible error in judgment. In the background the sounds of a party raged, but in the foreground was Giganto, also raging, and making it abundantly clear that his limited thought process had immediately determined that we were not wanted. After a brief verbal assault, the insane golem chased us back to the car, screaming and threatening, pounding on my car's roof with his fists, and in doing so encouraged us to flee the premises posthaste.

I relived that particular experience many times and always came to the same conclusion: it was right to flee with our tails between our legs. Though we outnumbered the unhappy Goliath three to one, we had, in fact, gone to his lair on our own accord, and in doing so had provoked his rage, as easy as that was. Plus, he was absolutely, incurably insane, and no one wants to mess with a lunatic. The lesson there, of course—do not go to a party at that guy's house.

Smack-Talking Bobby, Jehovah's Witless

Bobby was a strange bird—an awkward, socially retarded type—son of Jehovah's Witnesses whose parents my parents hid from when they came around to share or sell copies of *The Watchtower*. He was not a physical threat, but a verbal one, and his aggression came mainly in the form of taunts. I'd never thought much about him other than the fact that he sat in front of me in science class, but apparently my family's personal life was the topic at his family's dinner table. This became evident when he announced to the class that my mother, who had been suffering from breast cancer for a few years, "had her tit cut off."

We all have our trigger points—those that make us angry, those that make us furious, and those that send us hurtling over science tables trying to kill someone. That particular trigger point was instantly reached. The table that separated us proved no match for me; it was heavy and topped with equipment and made a tremendous racket when it fell, but it in no way inhibited my earnest attempt to strangle Bobby to death. My attempt at murder was interrupted by Andy, who pulled me, screaming and crying, off of Bobby, also screaming and crying. Though Andy had previously spent much of middle school taunting me, those taunts ended that day. I'd seemingly earned Andy's respect by trying to kill Bobby. It was a strange way to earn someone's respect, but I was happy to have it if it meant he'd stop calling me names in gym class.

Although I was suspended from school for three days, I was completely forgiven by my mother—which made me realize I had done the right thing. Ultimately, I was happy that I stood up for my mom and tried to strangle Bobby. Whether or not Bobby's family continued to chat about my mother's mastectomy at dinner I'll never know, for Bobby shut up after that. And that's the lesson there.

Burrito Boy, the Hungry Drunkard

Late one evening in Atlanta I found myself in a drive-through, sitting with my roommate in a line of automobiles. We'd had a post-pub hankering for Grade D meat rolled up in a processed flour shell, and this was the late-night establishment that catered to those particular cravings. The restaurant, like many fast-food restaurants, was situated smack-dab in the middle of a big parking lot, allowing the drive-through line to be fed from multiple directions.

As I approached the line of vehicles, I noticed another car full of passengers also interested in acquiring burritos, approaching from another direction. I believed I wanted burritos more, and cut their vehicle off preemptively. Although I beat them fair and square, the occupants of the other automobile disagreed, and the quarrel escalated to a can of beer being hurled at my car by one of that vehicle's unruly passengers.

This made me angry.

No doubt being liberated from fear by my aforementioned pub visit was the reason I chose to exit my vehicle and express my displeasure. This prompted the projectile launcher to exit his vehicle with great haste. As he raced toward me, I realized physical conflict was imminent. There was no time for diplomacy. As my assailant rounded the rear of the car and charged, I attempted to take him down with a swift karate-esque kick. The kind of kick that always works in your martial-arts class—when you rehearse it in slow motion.

For the record, karate kicks require sobriety and practice, both of which I was sorely lacking. He grabbed my leg, we both fell down, and began punching each other as everyone exited their vehicles to watch. I don't think a lot of time passed—it's hard to say when you're preoccupied with being punched in the head—but it seemed like a while. Eventually it occurred to me that we were fighting over burritos, something I managed to mention to the aggressor in between punching his head and being punched in mine. This registered and gave him cause for pause, leading to a cessation of hostilities. We sheepishly shook hands and went back to our vehicles—a victory for rational thought and diplomacy, albeit a little too late. Our détente was also no doubt encouraged by the realization that no one at the scene would have been eager to engage in field sobriety tests if the police stopped by.

The lesson here is obvious: Rushing into battle is never a good idea—especially when one has been drinking. That's because when one's been drinking, one is prone to squabble over things that might later appear trivial—such as burritos. Not to mention, one's limited knowledge of martial arts is rendered worthless after Guinness. The other lesson is, don't drink and drive, of course. Do as I say, not as I did.

Dan, the Victim Next Door

Dan was my closest neighbor and by default my occasional friend. My lack of friends in general made him valuable. What we lacked in relationship chemistry was made up for in convenience. We were both bored rural kids who spent afternoons wandering about our yards. I'd steal Dan's Matchbox cars, and he'd tell me the Jews killed Jesus. Every so often we'd run into Robert.

Robert lived not far away, a younger boy who was an opportunist when it came to bullying. If the scenario was right—if you were outnumbered—he would strike. But when he was outnumbered—such as the time my brother and I shoved grass clippings down his pants—he was helpless.

Robert had grown significantly since our last encounter. And he had a posse. He'd decided to use his newfound power for evil, and that meant picking on diminutive Dan. As the conflict escalated, I realized I had two options: I could run home and lose what I had of Dan's respect and friendship, or I could come to Dan's aid and improve upon it. Though I chose the latter, I was somewhat afraid of confronting Robert's posse directly—opting instead to scale a tree and throw a rock at him. My preemptive attack would come with no warning and even less thought to the possible consequences of my actions.

As unathletic as I was, it was actually a good throw. Solid, strong, direct. The only thing missing was my ability to aim. The rock struck Dan quite nicely on the side of the head. Robert, dumbfounded, stepped back. Where moments before there had been a loud engagement, there was now silence. That was short-lived, however, as a steady stream of blood shot out of Dan's head, and he began to wail like a professional banshee.

My boy, one way to defeat an enemy is to outright overpower them. That's a given. But another great way to defeat an enemy is to make your opponent think, or realize, that you are insane. No one wants to engage a nutcase, the key reason being they're unpredictable, unrestrained, crazy. Charles Manson might be small, old, and scrawny, but he's absolutely certified bonkers, and no one in their right mind would want to take him on in a fight. Likewise, as my friend Dan bled and wailed, it was obvious to Robert and his crew that I was a young, unstable man not to be trifled with. Anyone who was willing to stone his friend was trouble. The posse fled, and Dan, declaring that he couldn't see from one eye, screamed, bled, and began to stumble his way home. I descended the tree and followed, hoping beyond hope that parental authorities would somehow not be notified—a dream that was shattered the moment my mother looked out her window to see why Dan was screaming bloody murder.

I followed Dan as he screamed and flailed and ran home claiming that he'd been blinded. Fortunately this was only due to the copious amounts of blood in his eyes. The damage was temporary, though my handiwork required several stitches. To add insult to injury, the doctor's hydrogen peroxide bleached a section of his hair white—an embarrassment that lasted the bulk of the summer.

The lesson here is not to rush into things, lest your noble intentions backfire. My effort to rescue Dan was admirable, if not somewhat mitigated by cowardice. Had I stood shoulder to shoulder with my occasional friend, we both would likely have gone down together, but we'd have enjoyed the kind of camaraderie unique to soldiers. We might have even become better friends. In a sense it worked—I don't recall Robert troubling me after that. But Dan didn't much, either.

One hopes that as we progress into the twenty-first century, there will be fewer and fewer circumstances that warrant violence. I know that's a long shot, like winning the lottery or getting eaten by lions, but hope springs eternal. If you can take what I've told you and put it to good use, then there's a chance you won't find yourself in your late thirties, still bitter that you let some sadistic duffer crush your toes decades ago. That's an outcome worth fighting for.

Statistics show that 61.6%
of bullied children are
picked on because of
their looks or speech.
That's bad news for any
big-nose lisping zit face.

Humans are the only land
mammals that habitually
copulate face to face.
That and the ability to
philosophize and write
sitcoms is what sets us apart
from beagles and such.

5

We'll Need to Talk

My father told me all about the birds and the bees,
the liar—I went steady with a woodpecker
till I was twenty-one.

Bob Hope

Though not as terrible as blood cancer or lupus, one of the unfortunate downsides of aging is having to face unpleasant tasks in a responsible and mature manner. These tasks range from having to apologize for things we'd rather not apologize for, attending operas we'd rather not attend, and talking about subjects we'd rather not talk about.

Many years ago, while visiting friends in Ireland, I was chatting with Robert, the five-year-old son of my friend Rachel. Rachel was a single mother, a stigma to say the least in a land sown almost exclusively with Catholics. Nevertheless, she'd done a good job and had a lovely, bright, and articulate son who believed wholeheartedly that he knew where he came from.

Grandpa put an egg in Rachel's bum.

At some point Rachel was going to have to face her parental responsibilities and sit Robert down for a chat, lest

Robert continue to believe he came from an egg in his mom's behind, placed there by her dad no less. She was going to have to have the big talk and sort it all out. And at some point, so will I.

Assuming you're fairly normal—and frankly there are no guarantees of that because we share genes—there'll be a time when you, too, will have questions. I'll hopefully have answers for them. Answers that I'd better start preparing for, right about now.

The questions will center around your penis—which, at the moment, is a tiny stub. Really, it's a wee thing, which we've currently dubbed "lady-killer" because it's terribly funny when we ask where your lady-killer is and you point to your crotch. Never let it be said that parenting isn't without its entertaining perks.

Your penis's potential is currently unknown to you. Its utility strictly limited to what it seems that it's there for. Like a potted plant in a frat house, days go by when it gets no attention at all. And that's a great thing, really. I can say with certainty that your life right now is as happy-go-lucky and carefree as it can be for two reasons. One, you have no responsibilities up to and including wiping yourself. But the second and more important reason: you don't pay your little soldier any mind. You dream of tic tacs and lollipops and a stuffed duck you've named Caca. You scribble and dabble and get dirt caked under your fingernails, wholly free from animal impulses and impure thoughts. When you kiss a girl on the playground, there are no ulterior motives. You're not running for first base or laying any plans. Not a single calculation. For you, fantasies go no farther than pretending you're driving the shopping cart or acting like the cat.

Sure, there's the occasional moment of self-discovery that presents me with the parental catch-22: telling your child not to hump the tub will only encourage it. And is it so bad, anyway? Within moments you'll be distracted and move on to something else.

Overall, that teeny, tiny monster is as ineffective as the United Nations when it comes to exerting control. Why? Because you just don't care. And that, my little friend, is a blessing you won't appreciate until it's too late.

You can't fight nature. In due course, the hormones will fire up, and innocence will go out the window. But how great you have it now, what magnificent days they must be. How I long to not care about hints of nipple. What a joy to not be instinctively drawn to bared midriffs. Why must I be sidetracked by big bosoms, tight jeans, small bosoms, Asians, blondes, skirts? The mind reels to think how many hours, days, years one wastes chasing, drooling, gawking, longing—all because one day you realize that Mr. Tinkle isn't just for pee-pee anymore.

When that one day will come I can't say. There seems to be no set time for these things. No definitive age when I can expect to be asked what's up down there. No particular season when you're more or less likely to seek the answers that will get you banished from the Eden of childhood. There are many factors involved, you see. Your household environment. Your peers. How well I program the V-chip. It could come early on; it could come later on. But it will happen, and when it does, I'm not quite sure what to expect, although I will most likely be taken by surprise. If I know myself well enough, and I think I do because I'm me, I'll not know what to do. God help me if your mother's off running errands at the time.

It's hard to imagine what the moment will be like—when you'll choose to drop the bomb on me. Perhaps I'll be sitting at my desk in the evening, poring over papers and cursing this country's incomprehensible tax code. Maybe we'll be in the car on our way to patronize a giant retail chain. Or maybe it will be first thing in the morning. I'll be sipping from a cup of poorly brewed coffee and eating an inappropriate breakfast of hummus. You'll enter the room, we'll greet each other, then you'll cut to the chase and ask why Bridget makes your pee-pee tingle.

I apologize in advance for not knowing how I'll handle that. Chalk it up to the significance of the moment. At that point in time, we'll have moved into another chapter in our lives. A chapter where innocence is no longer assumed. Where slumber parties are now suspect. Where *Playboy* is no longer read for the articles. I'll realize you've grown, and that I have, too. In fact, I'll realize how rapidly I've grown because I'll suddenly have a child of my very own asking me why he wants to fondle Barbie rather than just pull her head off.

There is a lot riding on this inevitable discussion, which is why I want to start working on it now, preparation not being my strong point. It's an occasion I fear not being well equipped for. Say too little and you might walk away thinking babies come from an egg in the bum; say too much and twenty years later you're on *Oprah*—with boobs and a thong, going by the name Mizz Delicious.

When it comes to the Birds & Bees routine, I don't remember my own lecture at all, most likely because there wasn't one. Much of my childhood is a blur, and the blur doesn't seem to contain much reference to a sit-down session about my lady-killer. All my learning I did on my own as my mother spent the dawn of my sexuality sick with cancer. Dad, a young executive, was often away on business. In their defense, each probably thought the other had taken care of things and that I understood why I was so excited when I saw a Danish exchange student skinny-dipping. Unfortunately I was as naïve and ill-informed as an average college graduate.

Everything I wanted to know about sex but was afraid to ask, or simply wasn't told about, I learned from a dog-eared copy of *The Hite Report on Female Sexuality* that I found in my mother's night table. It wasn't the kind of book you would think to hide from your child, it being photo-free and clinical. Nothing but hundreds of women reporting what made them tick in the bedroom, or elsewhere. But the words were pornographic enough, and anyway, you take what you can get. It didn't take long for me to become hooked on these detailed accounts of women's sexual likes and dislikes, their hang-ups, their techniques. There were stories of first times, seductions and rapes, friends and neighbors, infidelity and debauchery. Everyone from prude to prostitute baring their soul, and everything else, to me. Although there wasn't one single photo to go with their stories, one paragraph alone was certainly enough to beat my mother's poorly-hidden copy of *Playgirl* or my father's attic stash of sterile 1960s lad mags. In the end, after numerous clandestine consultations with Ms. Hite's report, I felt I knew all there was to know. In particular, I learned some women satisfied themselves in the bath—a finding reinforced many years later by my upstairs neighbor's nightly endeavor of pleasuring herself in the tub. *Splish, splash, moan, moan.* It wasn't pretty, and neither was she.

But I digress. What matters here is not what I learned— it's too late for me—but what you'll learn. That falls on my shoulders, and so I really need to work out that whole speech. To answer the questions as informatively and evasively as possible. To tell you everything you need to know, but only exactly what you need to know. To determine what nuggets of wisdom I can part with, and what others you should find out on your own, or from friends at the pub. Or on dates. Is it my job to tell you some women masturbate in the bath? I think not.

This sex talk is no easy task. It's awkward and unpleasant. There's an air of "ick" about it, like someone imagining the details surrounding how he was conceived. Trust me, I shudder, too, as my father shuddered before me. No child wants to imagine the merger of Dad and Mom that led to the subsequent acquisition of child.

You should be warned that anything I do tell you, whatever speech I come up with, will most likely be riddled with inaccuracies and, of course, hypocrisy. Like the cop who rolls through stop signs and speeds home from work. I'll no doubt be better at telling you how to operate than doing so myself. Will I tell you that sex is what happens when a man and a woman are in love and care about each other? I'd be lying. I didn't love Maggie when she claimed my virginity. I liked her. Ditto Pam or Deborah or Debbie or Beth or Jodi or Judy or Sara or Sarah or Lakey or Anne or any of the others who made my pee-pee tingle. So to spare the hypocrisy, perhaps I should just be more honest: Son, sex is what happens between a man and a woman who are in love and care about each other. Or who work together late every Friday. Or who sat together on a plane. Or who live next door. Or who were drunk in a pub. I don't know. I really never gave it much thought. Don't forget I was schooled by a tawdry book of slutty stories posing as a scientific report.

I suppose I'll work it out in the end and give you the right answers to the right questions. At the very least, I'll endeavor to keep you from thinking you came from an egg in the bum.

There are several kinds of sex, son, but I'd argue the very best is when a man and a woman love each other—because that's where you came from.

Sorry to put that image in your head.

Events like Carnation Day and Valentine's Day are a great opportunity to remind the loners in school that no one is thinking of them.

6

There Is a Light at the End of the Tunnel

What does not kill me makes me stronger.

Nietzsche

I think it's fair to say that even parents who are not particularly skilled at the art of parenting want their children to enjoy a happy childhood. To that end, we subscribe to magazines like *Parenting* and read articles with titles like "Raising a Happy Child" and "How to Raise a Happy Child." We do things we wouldn't normally do, like attend the circus even though we're allergic to tigers and clowns frighten us to death, and we watch TV shows like *Dora the Explorer*—a young girl who shouts Spanish at you—and *The Wiggles*, four grown men singing about fruit salad and rose-addicted dinosaurs. We suffer through games of Chutes and Ladders, and we impulse-purchase stuffed penguins. We find ourselves clapping and cheering you on the toilet. It's fairly safe to say most parents would like their children to be happy as much as Bono would like to be Jesus.

Try as we may, however, there are no guarantees your childhood will be bright and cheerful. There are many factors out of our control—parents can get sick and die, classmates can be inherently evil, and we can fail to properly identify or value the sources of your angst and misery—either because we are out of touch as parents, or we just didn't realize how devastating it was when we forbade you from camping in a snowstorm. The fact of the matter is, a parent wants his child's wonder years to be idyllic and free from grief. No one wants to be responsible for producing a miserable lyricist or serial killer.

You would think that not being old enough to have regrets or responsibilities, and not needing to worry about finances or a career just yet would greatly help one be happy, but, alas, that's not the case. Childhood is a time when emotions are being tested, fears and phobias develop, personalities emerge. With all that come the trials and tribulations of youth: crushes go unreturned, friends steal our treasured eraser, bullies threaten and bruise us, and our favorite band breaks up. Add to that the ordeals of acne and puberty, and you have the foundations for despair, a burgeoning sense that life sucks, culminating with telling your parents you wish you'd never been born.

Despite the best efforts of my parents, I hated my childhood. My mother was terribly sick and later dying during my formative years—the weight of that distress was enough to send me to the school nurse nearly every day in eighth grade with blinding migraine headaches. To make matters worse, I was shy and awkward, a combination that ensured friends would be in short supply. And I lived in a house that seemingly radiated evil, as though it had been built on an old Indian burial ground. A horrifying picture of a malevolent clown hung over the dark, open basement, which I had to pass by every night on the way to bed. That basement was the source of countless nightmares, most of which involved a character named Poo Poo Man.

Poo Poo Man, as you might expect, was made of poo poo. And every night in my dreams he wanted to kill me in the basement via some ingenious method like a slide rigged with knives to stab me to death on the way down. Every night I would capitulate and tell Poo Poo Man he could kill me, but first I wanted to say good-bye to my mother, wherein I would plan my escape from his fecal clutches. And every night he would agree to that condition, probably because he had shit-for-brains. Though I thought I could rally my mother to save me, she would usually be busy washing the dishes. I would scream for help, but no sound would come out, and I'd tug at her leg, but she wouldn't notice. Poo Poo Man would slowly approach me, eager to take me to my doom in the basement. Inevitably I'd wake up screaming, another night's sleep ruined by a crap-covered demon. No doubt a dream analyst would have a field day with that plotline. At the time I believed I was tormented by Poo Poo Man because I lived in a haunted house with tasteless clown art. But I'm older now, and I realize it's because we had no air-conditioning.

Try as a parent may during the early years to make his or her child happy, there are no guarantees we'll go about doing it the right way. Sometimes we may even make matters worse. My father had the best of intentions when he reminded me, constantly, that I slouched, mumbled, and my lip stuck out. His well-meaning observations unfortunately did little for my meager self-esteem. I already felt like much of an outcast from frequently being reminded that I didn't have any friends. Eventually I did manage to find one—an angry, campy, strange boy who seemed destined for musical theater. Soon after I befriended him I was told I should perhaps have different friends.

I knew what was being implied when I was told it was strange not to have a girlfriend. I would have been happy to allay my father's fears, but the problem was that girls usually didn't like me, and my self-esteem was such that I was suspicious of any girl who did. Whether or not they were interested, I had the tendency to stumble all over myself in the presence of a female. At a middle-school party when Carolyn asked me to dance, I panicked and said no; then I went home and cried. When I was in high school, my father kept pressing me for a girlfriend until I finally met my very first one, in the McDonald's drive-through window. Apparently emboldened by my purchase of Chicken McNuggets, I threw the car in reverse and asked her out. I proudly brought her home to display to my father and quell his fears, only to have him knock on the bedroom door every time we closed it. Thus began a brief relationship that would eventually cost me my high-school ring, which I didn't really care about because I hated my nightmare high school.

What a child or young adult may interpret as an assault on his or her character or self-esteem is quite often just a parent's way of trying to be a good parent and make things better. Though we may send conflicting signals like, *You need friends, but not that one*, or, *Please don't be gay, but don't touch that girl*, we mean well. You can fault us for failure to deliver the message properly or tactfully, for accidentally spiking your heart with what we believe was constructive advice, but know that we have noble intentions. I will never actively set out to subsidize your melancholy. Just remember: most everything a parent does is well meaning, even if it confuses the hell out of you and makes you want to curl up and die. Consider that an invitation to ask for clarification when, like all fathers, I make a mistake and my best intentions backfire.

No matter what tribulations you may face in your youth, I want you to understand that as a child you are blessed with one thing that an adult doesn't have anymore: a lifetime ahead of you. It may be hard for a brokenhearted teen to imagine, but there is a light at the end of the tunnel. You should be aware that childhood experiences from the trivial to the nightmarish actually serve to build character. I can tell you this firsthand, having spent much of my youth despondent about my youth, hoping things would eventually be better, looking for the light at the end of the tunnel, which often turned out to be someone with a flashlight coming to tell me I was a loser.

In middle school, which I found traumatic and depressing, I longed for high school. There would be new people who hadn't yet judged me, who didn't know I was awkward and shy, lanky and clumsy, and generally hopeless with girls. Like Madonna, I could repackage myself and forget my regrettable past.

During the summer before high school, I attended Marine Military Academy. It was a boot camp for teens that my father had threatened to send me to because, like all teens, I was lazy and didn't want to do yard work early on a Saturday morning. In a rare moment of bravado, I took him up on his threat, and before long I was on a plane to Harlingen, Texas—an area known as the "hotbox" for reasons that became quite clear. My head was shaved, I was issued fatigues, and I began doing push-ups. Push-ups for marching out of step, push-ups for not speaking loud enough, push-ups for doing push-ups incorrectly. Push-ups because Greg talked back, push-ups because Wayne smiled, push-ups because Bravo Company got to the firing range faster.

While all of us were called maggots, we also had distinctive, personal nicknames. My fat roommate from Waco was Lard Bucket. In comparison, I got off easy. As the only Yankee there, I was Yankee and Yankee Boy and Boston Charles Winchester the Third. I was also called Vlad because when you shave my head I look like Nosferatu.

By the time I left Marine Military Academy's summer camp, I was, as they'd say in the Marines, gung ho. Although it wasn't long before I stopped waking up at 6 a.m. and lost my enthusiasm for spontaneous push-ups, I still retained my military zeal. It was part of the New Me, and unfortunately was the reason one of my first high-school essays was about napalm, burning flesh, and scattered bodies. I was soon dubbed a freak, and upon the realization that I'd blown my chance to repackage myself, my heart sank. I realized that like middle school, high school was going to suck.

I spent most of my lunches hidden in the upper balcony of the empty auditorium. In some respects it was a good choice—I saved lots of money by not eating and retained my lanky, awkward figure. As I sat there, alone, riding out the lunch period every day, I quietly hoped things would get better. That there would be something to live for and look forward to. And there was. It was called college, and there I was able to develop a personality I not only could live with, but actually kind of liked despite a lingering immaturity. I found friends who'd be part of my life until the end. I was able to have girls in my room, and close the door, and my father didn't knock on it and ask me what I was doing. All the hardships of my earlier years, the seemingly insurmountable awkwardness, loneliness, and despair, was mountable after all. Being different was no longer a curse; it was a blessing. Finally, I felt comfortable in my own skin. If a girl asked me to dance, I wouldn't panic, say no, and go home crying. I would panic and say no because I can't dance.

And so the gist is this: Though I can assure you much effort will be put into you having a happy and rewarding childhood, like any parent I cannot guarantee it. Happiness can be elusive as you find your way in the world, but know that the slings and arrows suffered in your youth, those things that may seem like the end of the world to you, are only building character. The relationships you'll cry over, the traumas perceived and real, you'll overcome them. Even terrible ordeals that can only be expressed with a hastily scribbled montage of sappy song lyrics.

Although I had no shortage of moments when I wished I had never been born, ultimately I'm glad I was. Because if I hadn't been, you wouldn't have been, and that would be tragic for both of us, indeed.

Having a positive
attitude can really
separate you from
the other inmates
on death row.

Adolf Hitler wanted to be
an architect, but failed
the entrance exam at the
architectural school in Vienna.
Then he went on to conquer
Europe and kill millions. The
lesson: Never lose hope.

7

Your Career

I've missed more than nine thousand shots in my career.
I've lost almost three hundred games. Twenty-six times
I've been trusted to take the game winning shot and
missed. I've failed over and over and over again
in my life. And that is why I succeed.

Michael Jordan

I must confess to having been fundamentally clueless about
career paths and possessing in my youth nothing more than
a vague idea of what I wanted to do, with absolutely no concept of how such a dream could be realized. This is in stark
contrast with those who emerge from the womb with a cover letter and seem to have their lives mapped out; their first
million scheduled for eight years after they graduate Harvard cum laude. Harvard, of course, coming only after they
achieve high-school valedictorian and join the military for
two years, to add leadership to their résumé.

I envy those individuals who seem to have been plot-
ting their professional trajectory in between having their

bottoms wiped. Those individuals who entered their teens as if steered by some sort of supernatural guidance counselor that conferred upon them a wisdom and foresight beyond their years. How a thirteen-year-old knows what exactly he needs to do to get where he wants to go, much less has the interest in doing so, is beyond me. At thirteen I was merely discovering the trappings of puberty—which you'll learn is primarily pimples and frustration. But these other people—these strange, unnaturally motivated sorts—were already working toward glorious résumés that would need no padding, and were well on the path to a quarter-page *New York Times* obit in sixty years. Those people don't seem to be in such large supply as the other people—the ones who think they want to do this, or maybe that. The ones who aren't sure where Point A is and for whom Point B is eternally a dot on the horizon no matter how hard they paddle.

I hope that my experiences as an occupational nomad and my limited knowledge of the success tracks of others can benefit you—whether you find yourself having a strategy early on or if, like me, you simply find yourself subject to serendipity, occasionally pointing to something and saying, "Okay, I'll try that now."

From what I can discern, luck, talent, and motivation are the three factors that will define your career's overall success. Large quantities of all three virtually guarantee you a rewarding career, with the rewards diminishing as the three factors do. Some luck, some talent, and some motivation can still lead to some measure of career success. No luck, no talent, and no motivation, and you may very well find yourself trapped in a hammock, or house-sitting for O. J. Simpson.

Luck comes in the form of sheer chance that increases our potential for success. This could be anything from being born into a political dynasty, or a record executive hearing your amazing rendition of "Sussudio" on a subway platform. Right place, right time, divine providence, or finding yourself in the shower with Harvey Weinstein—all examples of success-enhancing luck.

Talent goes without saying, really. The ability to mesmerize audiences with a flute, pick the right stocks, hit effortless home runs, or write the songs that make the young girls cry. All examples of talents that will enhance your career success.

Motivation was described to me once by a very old, very famous television star who was trying to pick me up in an airport lounge in St. Louis. "It's a fire in the belly," he said, before he invited me over. "You know it when you have it." And while I may shudder at the memory of an old man coming on to me, he had a good point. That fire— the one in the belly and not the old man's pants—is the determination that motivates us to practice when we'd rather sleep, to subject ourselves to fruitless audition after fruitless audition, to spend our Friday nights poring over legal loopholes in the hopes of getting our murderous client off.

You needn't have all three factors to succeed in your career—two will suffice if they're significant enough. For example:

An aspiring actor desperate for fame, whose mother is a well-known casting director has motivation and luck and really needs no talent.

An unbearable chef who has dedicated his life to being Hitler with a whisk, has motivation and talent and needs little luck.

An artist who paints angry tirades about his uncle that gets discovered by the Tate Gallery has talent and luck and needs no motivation.

Regardless of your factor levels, far be it from me to point you in any particular career direction. Your choice should come from the heart, and whether that means following the footsteps of your father or forging your own path, you have to do what you want to do. And if what you want to do is follow your father's footsteps, I pity you, because your father's footsteps meander like those of a blind, disoriented aborigine on a walkabout.

In my unprofessional life, I have been a waiter, advertising writer, grip and sound man, voice actor, principal, stand-in, commercial actor, interior decorator, casting director, producer, radio character, humorist, television commentator, and apparently, author. Most everything by complete accident.

I owe it all to a game plan that was not so much a game plan as it was a vague sense of direction. Luckily for you,

72

this is not a genetically acquired trait. I am the son of a man who had it all figured out before he was weaned off training wheels.

Being a creative type, I attended college for film because I had an interest in film, and that was pretty much my whole plan. I hadn't worked the rest of it out yet, but somehow had decided a degree in film would open doors somewhere, probably. Maybe. I wasn't alone, of course. With the exception of a few students who would have the advantage of industry connections—the son of a filmmaker, the daughter of a Hollywood bigwig—we were on our own, or would be in four short years.

Some who graduated ahead of us did have a game plan, or so they thought. Todd obtained the fax number for a film studio, and every day would send them a page from a script he had written. The idea was that Hollywood executives would be huddled around their facsimile, eagerly awaiting the next screenplay morsel. After weeks of faxing, Todd followed up with a phone call to introduce himself as the author of the work. "Don't ever call here again," he was told.

It would seem that part of the battle comes down to how your brain works. There are business minds, and there are creative minds. Those blessed with a business mind seem to set goals. They reach those goals, and they set new goals, reach those goals, and so on and so forth.

Creative minds are different. Creative minds have goals like, "My name is Bob Smith. I would like to be Steven Spielberg. Thank you."

Business minds are blessed with career savvy. They're prepared to answer fearlessly when asked what their salary demands are. They look their employer straight in the eye and with supreme confidence tell them exactly what they want, and the employer nods. They read contracts and negotiate severance pay and perks like company cars and expense accounts.

Creative minds are cursed with insecurity and doomed to be flappable. Ask them what their salary demands are, and they'll hem and haw and sheepishly ask what *you* think they're worth. When you tell them, even though it breaks their heart, they say, "When do I start?" They pay as much attention to contracts as a stage mom does to her child's emotional development. Creative minds often confuse an expense account with an $8 per diem.

When I started my first salaried job, the $18,500 they offered prompted my employer to ask, "Why the long face?"

"I just thought it would be more," I whimpered.

"You're getting $500 more than the usual junior copywriter," he responded.

Sold. That was all I needed to hear.

To succeed in the career you want, one of the smartest things you can do is get to know people who are doing what you'd like to be doing. After all, a professor can teach you about screenwriting or economics, but only a screenwriter or economist can show you how the door actually opens. Ask questions to see what they did—and hope that what they did doesn't involve you going back in time and joining the army, or getting a doctorate from Oxford. Know that there are multiple paths into any career. Some easier than others. And find inspiration in Tori Spelling's claim that she got a job on her dad's show without any help from her dad.

Friends and acquaintances are the next best thing to having family in the business you want to be in. Don't be afraid or too proud to tap them for help if they're in a position to do so. For ages I was afraid to ask my friend about his work as a writer on *The Daily Show with Jon Stewart*. I didn't want him to feel like I was stepping on his toes. I didn't want him to think I was using him. When it finally occurred to me that it would be okay to ask for his assistance after all, he was more than helpful. All my fears that he'd react angrily were unfounded and foolish. He encouraged me and showed me what I needed to do, offered guidance that no one outside the show could offer. Thanks to him, I knew exactly what they would like and more importantly, wouldn't like. What would fly and what would fail. It was a most enviable position for me. I had a valuable "in." And then I waited too long, finally deciding to go for it at the very same time he decided to leave the show. My in was out, and so was I. And how did he get his job in the first place? Through a friend, of course.

Whether you have a business mind or a creative mind, whether you've figured it all out or find yourself standing on the seashore wondering how to become a pirate, I can offer you one piece of advice that is universally true: Absolutely nothing will happen without some effort on your part. I can't fault you for not having a game plan, but for any kind of success, you'll at least have to play.

The biggest cause of matrimonial fighting is money, so make sure to always carry large wads of cash around the house.

8

You Can't Take It with You

I acquired more wealth, power, and prestige than most.
But you can acquire all you want and still feel empty. What
power wouldn't I trade for a little more time
with my family? What price wouldn't I pay
for an evening with friends?

Lee Atwater

When a 320-pound man plagued with eczema wants to be spanked by a gorgeous Czech girl, no amount of begging or pleading is going to make that happen. He might ask nicely, yell, or even weep a river, but the only way he's going to get what he wants is if he has some money. Behold, the mighty power of the dollar.

Five thousand years ago, when a pharaoh died, the Egyptians buried him with furniture, food, tools, pleading servants, and lots of gold—all things intended for use in the afterlife. Today, that crap is still sitting there. Proof positive that you cannot take it with you.

And so here you have money's great paradox: On the one hand, a vile glutton with a flaky, freshly spanked bottom suggests money's intrinsic value. On the other hand, a solid-gold dining set leans against a sarcophagus, covered in five millennia-worth of dust—proof of money's ultimate insignificance.

The truth of the matter is, money falls somewhere in between blessing and curse, acting both as hero and as the diametrically opposed evil twin that inevitably appears in any long-running television series. Money is like a handgun: It can persuade, intimidate, and give one a false sense of self-worth. It can save you or ruin you, depending on how you handle it. And anyone who leaves it lying around the house is asking for trouble.

Money has been around quite a long time, existing in many different forms, many of which were edible. Whether the accepted legal tender was corn, salt, gold, cows, bread, shells, rum, or paper, the idea has always been the same: I will give you this if you will give me that. It no doubt outdates the world's oldest profession; obviously money had to come before any prostitute would.

Though mankind has gotten older and wiser and since invented the wheel, electricity, and reality television, the fundamental concept of money has remained as unchanged as Dick Clark. There is simply no better way to motivate someone to collect our trash, mow our lawns, and check our prostates.

Like it or not, you'll need money to function in today's society. You'll need more of it to function with a nicer watch, and even more of it if you want a mansion to hold functions in. But to lead a happy and rewarding life, you'll need to understand money's potential to misguide you and pilot you to mischief. Be advised, money is dangerous. It has the potential for trouble—like an unmonitored Michael Jackson at your slumber party. Money can harm you just as easily as it can get you a lap dance from a woman named Karma.

There's no foreseeable alternative to money—good news for cashiers, attorneys, and wallet makers; bad news for college communists and the late John Lennon. Still, it doesn't stop people from dreaming. For far too long I had a roommate with a well-rehearsed "World Without Money" theory. Lubricating him with a few pints guaranteed the theory would be passionately presented to everyone in the room. Usually the room was a bar.

The "World Without Money" was a simple dream—a long-haired, unemployed man's dream that one day there would be a world free from the oppression of having to acquire capital. Not just the distribution of wealth, but the elimination of it. In this world, you wouldn't need a wallet or an ATM card or even a tip jar. You would simply do what you wanted and take what you wanted. Bruce would make boats because he liked to make boats—getting his parts for free from Carl, who liked to make boat parts for some reason. If Alice liked to bake bread, she would do just that, using free flour from Marvin, who loved to farm and mill wheat. If Doug wished to design castles, he would do so. And so on and so forth—everybody doing what they loved to do for free.

If Alice the Baker wanted a boat, she'd just ask Bruce the Shipwright for one. When Doug the Architect got hungry designing a citadel for Marvin's wheat farm, he'd hit Alice up for a baguette. The world functioned on people doing what they enjoyed. Unburdened by the tyranny of capital, there would be no greed and everyone would be happy. All would be well with the world. It was a novel idea, but it was the brainchild of an unemployed film-school graduate who memorized *The Simpsons* in between bong hits. In the end, the "World Without Money" was just another stoner fantasy—naïve silliness masquerading as high philosophy. It failed to consider that money actually served as a powerful incentive for getting things done. No one in their right mind would want to clean your house or change adult diapers for free. If his deficient dream were ever realized, we'd have all the free boats and baguettes we needed, but our filthy castles would smell like Grandpa's crap.

So, until bartering comes back in vogue, or some dictator emerges from a cloud of hashish smoke to impose the "World Without Money" on us, money is here to stay. Therefore, I think it's best you know a little bit about it—so that you might wind up neither sleeping on a park bench nor dying alone in one-thousand-thread-count sheets.

It's a common misperception that money is evil. Garbage. Money isn't evil. Money is indifferent, like the Swiss. Call it a dollar or a pound or a ruble or a yen, but it is merely a tool that can be used for good, bad, or purchasing a complicated latte. Frankly, money doesn't care if it goes to a children's charity, buys a friend yogurt, or ruins your marriage. It just sits. If you're smart it sits in an interest-bearing account that is keeping up with inflation. If you're not smart, it sits in an interest-bearing account in Nigeria, after you've e-mailed a complete stranger with your personal details.

How you acquire money is up to you. It's a given that some methods are more lucrative than others. Teaching, though noble and important, often pays minimally; meanwhile, taking the helm of a megacorporation and driving it into the ground is exceedingly lucrative. Policemen get shot at for low pay while Orlando Bloom seduces hot chicks and gets millions of dollars. If it sounds unfair, that's because it very well may be. But money isn't everything, and I hope you will pursue a line of work that is personally rewarding first and financially rewarding second. That said, it's worth knowing that you will probably not make a lot of money if you find wearing a sandwich board personally rewarding.

There is not necessarily a relation between hard work and return on investment. One man may toil all his life, living paycheck to paycheck, while another retires at twenty-four after registering the domain hotteenfarmsex.com. There are many factors that influence what is and isn't in your bank account. Some you have no control over, like inheritance and luck. Others you do—like avoiding slot machines, get-rich-quick hucksters, and taking advantage of double coupons.

How you acquire money says a lot about you as a person. There are good and bad ways, of course. Usually the bad ways involve bloodshed or felonies. If you acquire money at the expense of others—such as being a trial lawyer who advertises on a bus—that suggests a failure in character. There's no sense in being rich if you're morally bankrupt. At the end of the day, you should be able to feel good about yourself and the money you have; no one should want to kill you or put you in jail. One should never sacrifice his or her reputation or principle for profit. Deep down we all know this. Nevertheless, money often makes people foolish and shortsighted. Greed subjugates civility. Friendships collapse, families implode, lives are ruined. Sometimes people even die. Prisons are chock-full of greedy dimwits who took out insurance policies on their wives and killed them before realizing this was a fairly standard story line on Court TV.

Money will often try to control you, to be the defining force in your life. Take Gollum in *The Lord of the Rings*. Gollum gets demented over a ring, focusing all his time and energy on obtaining it. This changes him into something dark and evil, blinded by greed on a single-minded quest. In this way he is very much like an investment banker.

Ultimately Gollum's greed consumes him. Having betrayed his friends and exhausted all good in him, the wretch finally acquires his precious treasure only to plummet into the lava at the appropriately named Mount Doom. One more life squandered by avarice. Let that be a lesson to you. And let that also be advice to avoid hiking any place called Mount Doom. Pity their tourist bureau.

We're often misled into believing that having lots of money will solve all our problems and make everything better. History is filled with sad souls who believed more money and more things could cure them of their melancholy. Money is the solution in some respects—if our problem is paying our college debts or buying a meticulously crafted German vacuum—but money is modern snake oil. It's no cure for depression, emptiness, or malaise. You can be just as unhappy in a Bentley as you can in a Buick. The chronic redecoration of your summer home suggests more of a problem with you than your drapes.

You can seek solace in Prada, and while you'll enjoy the fine craftsmanship and superior materials, you can still be left wanting. That's because money can change your environment, your look, your income bracket, and your breasts, but it will ultimately not put a smile on your face or warm your heart. Just look at the ads for designer labels and all you see is high-maintenance humans scowling and staring off into the distance. For once, truth in advertising.

You don't need a lot of money to be happy, so don't fool yourself into thinking that you do. The first girl to shatter my heart was lovely and poor and lived in a home with a roof that was stitched together, barely keeping the place from being condemned. They were a large, well-behaved, and sweet family, and at night they gathered in the living room to hear Dad play the piano while Mom sang. The piano wasn't a Steinway and the wine they sipped was too sweet and came from a jug. But that didn't matter. When all was said and done, they had a better life than many of the dour mannequins cluttering the Hamptons. What are the supermarket tabloids and society pages anyway but a *Who's Who* of the dysfunctional rich?

Don't let money deceive you. As attractive as you may be, if you're eighty-nine and a centerfold is coming on strong, look around and see if you're standing on your yacht. Money can't buy you love, but it can buy you someone who loves money. Use money to get the girl and you will get the girl you deserve.

And don't let money cloud your judgment or mores. Tough to do in a culture that places so much emphasis on a buck. We're often guilty of hypocrisy, holding the moneyed to a different, lower standard than the unwashed. A poor man who neglects his kids is reviled as an absentee dad, while a rich man who does the same is hailed as a workaholic. A common girl who's perpetually on all fours may be a trashy slut, but add an inheritance and a publicist to the equation and she's an heiress. Our often misguided respect for the wealthy is why no one has called Donald Trump out for having a multi-million-dollar home decorated like a Romanian bordello.

Speaking of brass and mirrors, don't assume money means class. One of the great realities in this land of opportunity is that background and lineage are not obligatory for success. There's no caste system to doom you at birth; no royal bloodline—aside from the Kennedys. Be you from the ghetto or prairie, there is no established protocol for becoming a wealthy American. That's a wonderful thing, indeed, giving us the rags-to-riches stories that define the American dream. Sadly it also means Courtney Love can afford to live in your condo, and you might find yourself in a five-star restaurant seated next to Snoop Dogg's eighty-man entourage.

Judge a man by the content of his character, not his portfolio, and realize that money oftentimes deserves respect as much as it deserves contempt. It's important and it's not. You can have a fulfilling life with little, and a horrible life with a lot. It can be a great friend and formidable foe.

And never forget, you can't take it with you. Especially if you're trying to leave Las Vegas.

Drunk Finns can be interesting because many of their grandfathers fought for the Nazis. So they get tipsy and apologize a lot.

9

Get Up, Get Out, and Go Where the Toilets Are Different

> The world is a book and those who do not travel
> read only one page.
>
> *Saint Augustine (354–430)*

Saint Augustine's wise words come from a time when traveling was more often than not a treacherous ordeal involving barbarians, donkeys, and brushes with death. While today we complain about leg room and post-9/11 screening procedures, travelers of yesteryear had to deal with various plagues, and maps as accurate as Ray Charles playing darts. Nevertheless, they understood the importance of not staying in one place, of putting on a decent pair of shoes—if they had any—and exploring the world outside their hamlet. What was true in the days long before Expedia, mileage programs, and Samsonite is still true today: Travel is enlightenment, and enlightenment is knowing that Jamaica sucks, Chinamen eat bees, and a French guy is going to try to sleep with your wife.

Now, that kind of enlightenment may sound like a sweeping generalization, but it isn't. It's an *educated* sweeping generalization arrived at only after one has made the effort to travel—to read more than one page, as Saint Augustine said. Particularly the page about French guys circling your wife like crazed hyenas. Really, it's that bad.

I love to travel, and I hope you'll love to travel, too. Dragging luggage to strange places frees us from our mundane existence and opens new doors behind which are many things to amaze, amuse, and confound. Like squat toilets. Having detoured from your day-to-day routine, your senses are in overdrive; everything is new, alien, in the moment—and as such, wholly stimulating. Imagine the thrill and excitement of being able to look toward every point on the compass and not see a single Starbucks.

Traveling gives us the ability to not only see new sights, but to be new people. To stagger back to our Dublin hostel and pass out buck naked. To wake late the next day covered in Grandma's brownies—a going-away gift we'd mistaken for a pillow. To lie there, naked and alone in a cheap bunk bed thousands of miles from home, and slowly realize that everyone in the hostel saw you on their way out. Thanks to travel, what would ruin our reputation at home is just another schmuck abroad who drank fourteen pints of Guinness.

Traveling is a college in and of itself. One where the textbooks are menus and street signs, the campus is the ruins of an abbey, and the professor is an old man blowing his nose into his hands before he makes your falafel. We go, we experience, we ask questions, and we learn. Then we get back home to make sweeping generalizations about Asian hygiene and dwarfen Frenchmen trying to bed our wives.

Traveling alters our perspectives and shatters our preconceived notions; unless our preconceived notions were that Belgium is boring and Poland drinks too much. Had I not gone to China, I'd never have known they had Ferrari dealers, something seemingly incompatible with the concept of a classless worker's paradise. But I went and I saw, and having done so, I can say firsthand that Chinese people *can* buy Ferraris. But they can't drive them. And they eat sautéed bee pupae and bamboo worms. They don't like cheese. They storm the elevator. They believe in dragons. And they don't listen. Tell a Chinese peddler no, and she'll follow you the length of the Great Wall until you buy her postcard. I know all these things only because I traveled.

It was travel that gave me an education in the power of advertising. I'd been sold the idea of Jamaica being a sun-drenched paradise with carefree natives smiling and frolicking to a Bob Marley sound track on a pristine beach. Having been there, I know it's a tropical hellhole with barbed wire, teen whores, and people trying to braid your hair by force. I can tell you firsthand that Norwegian men and women are gorgeous. But liquor one up, and they'll bore you to death with stories of their tiresome Viking past. A whole country obsessed with rapists in horn hats. However, that's still preferable to watching Italian men trying to pinch women's asses all day. That's an uncomfortable spectacle, much like a German girl's unshaven armpit.

These generalizations are not unfair. They're based on experiences gained through travel. And anyway, foreigners make sweeping generalizations about us, too. One visit to New York, and they assume America smells like pee. They're convinced we're all fat, gun-toting louts. And they think we're all stupid, just because some lady from Long Island tried to rent a car in Venice. Son, you should know that even your own mother, within minutes of our first encounter in Paris, declared to me her belief that Americans were obnoxious—a belief that stemmed from her own personal travel experiences. To Mexico. Where everyone sits around and says gringos suck, in between guacamole and siestas.

Heed Saint Augustine's advice. Travel. It offers you empowerment. If you're not speaking from firsthand experience, you're simply relaying something you read somewhere, or overheard at the next urinal. Travel gives you credibility. Your message of lecherous Frenchmen, scary Icelandic women, or India's filth is far more powerful if you've been there and experienced it in person. That's because you're an eyewitness. Someone with a first-person account of a mousy Parisian chasing your lady into the restroom, a wild-eyed Icelander threatening all the men in the room, and a guy dying from a poop-covered apple in New Delhi.

When you travel, even something as routine as trying to get clean becomes educational. Squatting in a curtainless shower with a broken hose drooling tepid water on us would be unacceptable at home, sure, but abroad? It's another mind-opening experience in the City of Lights. We become Socrates; we ask questions. Shouldn't there be a shower curtain to keep water from getting everywhere? Don't they have hot water? Where's my wife?

The answers are yes, no, and getting molested in the Louvre.

Learning like this wouldn't happen while sitting in the comfort of our living rooms, with our HDTVs, our boxed wine, our reliable "electricity." It takes traveling to realize that lots of hot Thai girls are actually hot Thai guys.

Had I not been traveling, I'd never have stayed in a cheap hostel in the red-light district of Vienna. Had I not stayed in a cheap hostel in the red-light district of Vienna, I'd never have been approached by a Viennese hooker. Had I not told a Viennese hooker I was broke and trying to call my dad, she'd never have invited me into her whorehouse to use the phone. And if you've never called your dad from a Viennese whorehouse to tell him everything's okay, you're missing out on a great memory. And I owe it all to travel.

Let us not forget, either, son, that your entire existence is due to the fact that your mother and I were travelers. Had I not been trying to satisfy my wanderlust and lust-lust, I'd never have found myself trying to steal a Polish girl from an Iranian man in an Irish bar in Paris. Travel not only increases your repertoire of cultural anecdotes, but also the odds of you getting lucky.

Fortunately, we've come a long way from Saint Augustine's time when "bon voyage" meant "hope you make it back." It's easier and cheaper than ever to experience the world so that we might visit far-off places and leap to fairly broad but seemingly accurate conclusions. There's no excuse not to go. People traveled long before Fodor's, Dramamine, and Virgin made it less painful, yet we complain about layovers, airline food, and antiquated elevators.

Should the urge hit us to watch naked Brazilians dance on floats, see an Irishman fight and love the same man in a three-minute span, or be kidnapped by Columbian rebels, we can act on a moment's notice. After only a handful of hours of abuse at the hands of semicompetent airport security and airline personnel, we can arrive in a completely different airport in a completely different country with a completely different culture. Like France, for example, a place where everyone looks forward to settling down with a wife. Preferably yours.

And that's what I'm hoping to impart, really. Before you can make sweeping generalizations about an entire culture, you must endeavor to experience that culture firsthand. Only after you have done so will you be truly qualified to disparage their inferior ways, mock their forms of entertainment, gag on their foods, curse their lifestyles, and laugh at their traditions.

So, listen to Saint Augustine. He's old and very dead, but his wisdom aged quite well. Get out there and turn a few pages. Then come back, appreciate what you've got, and tell your wife you don't want her talking to any more Frenchmen. Sure, it's a sweeping generalization, but if you've actually traveled there, fended off the natives, and labored to pronounce *croissant* correctly, you've earned the right to make it.

Only 4 percent of the U.S. population is vegetarian, but they're easily identifiable because they look pale and curse your leather boots.

10

Gray Is Good

The color of truth is gray.

André Gide

College is often a time of great change for an individual. They're away from home for the first time, no longer under the direct supervision of their parents, and at liberty to adopt personas and values that they'd be quick to deny or admonish if they lived at home. I was no exception. Within minutes of arriving at college, I was well on my way to becoming a righteous, unbearable, extremist botheration.

Nobody likes an extremist. Whether they're screaming at you for driving a car, screaming at you for not believing in their deity, or screaming at you for wearing a fur coat, an extremist inevitably becomes tiresome—even if they do offer some kind of initial amusement. This is because most people simply don't like to be screamed at and told they're doing something wrong all the time.

My transformation to annoying extremist started under the influence of a band called The Smiths, which was helmed by an opinionated, seemingly unhappy man who went by the name of Morrissey. I was introduced to the band by my first love, Lynn, the girl who would go on to break my heart not long into my first year of college.

Morrissey sang songs that were as melancholy as they were witty, songs with titles like "Heaven Knows I'm Miserable Now" and "The Queen Is Dead." They were antipop ballads filled with angst and despair. In some strange way they were uplifting—probably because you felt better by not being him.

One song in particular caught my attention. I listened to it over and over again and even went so far as to pound out the lyrics on my typewriter—a device that, like the Walkman, was once considered cutting edge. Whenever you go to the trouble to transcribe a song's lyrics, that's a good indication the song is important to you.

The song was "Meat Is Murder," and unsurprisingly it was a call to action for vegetarianism. Morrissey was a self-described celibate vegetarian, eschewing both sentient bed partners and foodstuffs. I had no interest in being celibate, but I did take Morrissey's other passion to heart. I officially joined the struggle against bovine oppression when I taped the lyrics to the door of my dorm room and stopped eating hamburgers.

As soon as I stopped eating meat, I made sure everyone knew that I'd done so, and was, therefore, morally superior. Letting everyone know you're morally superior is called activism.

Naturally, since I'd chosen to make a big stink about not eating meat, many people were inclined to ask why I'd stopped eating meat. That was my cue to let them know I believed meat was murder and had the lyrics to back that argument up.

This would then prompt some folks to ask if I believed eating chicken and fish was murder as well. Naturally the answer had to be "yes," even though Morrissey hadn't exactly said so. In order to preserve the moral high ground, or in fact gain even more moral high ground, I soon stopped eating chicken and fish altogether, telling folks, "If it walks, talks, swims, or squawks, I won't eat it."

This was not an easy thing to do. In the late 1980s, vegetarianism was far from mainstream and still fairly awkward. Being vegetarian often meant you didn't eat *as much* meat or you avoided veal because of the cruel conditions the calf was raised under, but to not eat any meat, chicken, or fish pretty much condemned you to tofu. Tofu's claim to fame was—and presumably still is—that it took on the flavor of whatever you cooked it with. For the record, so does sawdust. Tofu sucked in 1986, and twenty-some years later it still sucks. As a new vegetarian in those less accommodating times, I found myself eating a great deal of pasta and salad.

Now that I was fully vegetarian, I began to build myself a moral citadel atop the moral high ground I had taken. That enabled me to annoy even more people. As I soon discovered, when you're so amazingly morally superior to others, they will be inclined to challenge your devotion. They wasted no time attacking my position. Did I wear leather shoes? Did I have a leather belt? If meat was murder, wasn't belt murder? Wasn't shoe murder? They had a valid argument. In short order I was wearing canvas belts and shoes and keeping my money in a nylon wallet.

Though my shoes were pitifully ugly and offered no insulation in the winter, I had successfully countered any suggestion that I wasn't wholly committed to my cause. My feet were rotting in my lousy shoes, but I was at least proving a point to my detractors. Armored in natural fibers and from the top of my moral citadel, I was able to look down on people for being carnivores, for wearing leather jackets or fur-lined gloves. They had nothing on me, until they started asking about my shampoo.

Was I using anything that contained animal by-products or was tested on animals? Was my lunch accidentally contributing to the suffering of animals? If so, I was guilty of being a hypocrite, they'd say. Fighting words. In no time I found myself scouring product labels for the key words and chemical compounds that suggested ingredients of a dubious nature. Suddenly words like *lanolin* were evil. I agonized over purchases, wondering if the company that made my shaving cream might possibly have tested it on a rabbit at some point in their ninety-year history. Dining out became a nightmare. Was the griddle contaminated by meat juice? Were my fries cooked in lard? Was there chicken stock in the vegetable soup? One question after another that no doubt had my waiter wondering why I'd left the house in the first place. Certainly I could have spared everyone the misery of my presence by just staying home and cooking tofu with something it could assume the flavor of.

From the comfort of my seemingly impregnable moral citadel, I began to reinforce my position even more. I read books like Peter Singer's *Animal Liberation* and began to practice rebuttals to the challenges that were frequently posed to me. The next natural step was for me to join People for the Ethical Treatment of Animals. PETA was filled with well-meaning, sensitive people like me who were hell-bent on annoying everyone. They have strong views on all things related to animals—eating them, raising them, having them as pets, and especially animal experimentation. They call it vivisection, for obvious reasons: It sounds much more ominous. I was a good little PETAn. They sent me literature that reinforced my beliefs, and I dutifully spread it all over my campus. I subscribed wholeheartedly to whatever they said. Humans weren't meant to eat meat? Sure, no problem. Cow milk is bad for you? Okay, I'll buy that. I took hard-line stances on issues and refused to budge. If your uncle had cancer that could be cured by killing three sheep, I'd have said no, because I believed the sheep's lives were just as valuable as your uncle's.

My views were extreme. I fantasized about shadowy groups like the Animal Liberation Front and wondered if I, too, shouldn't be out there setting fire to laboratories, freeing rats, and threatening scientists. Fortunately I didn't have that much time on my hands and limited my activism to being a thorn in the side of mostly friends and acquaintances.

But my all-or-nothing extremist approach didn't sit right with me. Gradually I began to be troubled. Conflicted. I had doubts. Like a homophobic evangelist dating a gay masseur, I found myself living a lie. I loved animals, sure, but I also loved steak, to be honest. I still believed testing eyeliner on rabbits was wrong, but if finding the cure for cancer was going to take some rats . . . they were rats. The way veal was raised was still appalling, and I refused to order it, but a free-range chicken? Yummy. I no longer saw everything in black and white. It was a major revelation: everything was gray. For the first time I started to ask myself questions about my own views, to doubt some of the things I would have fallen on the sword for not long ago. Aren't humans actually omnivores? Is milk really poisonous? Is setting a laboratory on fire and risking human lives in the name of animal liberation an act of heroism, or terrorism?

Of course, now my intractable position as an extremist had forced me to remain a vegetarian far longer than I actually wanted to be. I'd gotten so used to standing on the moral high ground, lecturing people and shaking my head, that I didn't quite know how to get down with my pride intact. If I had only shut up at the very beginning and kept everything to myself, I could have simply made a quiet change and started snacking on cold cuts. Instead I found myself a closet meat-eater, continuing my facade as an animal avenger, yet coveting my neighbor's ribs. A few beers in me and I'd be eyeing someone's basket of wings as I picked through another boring salad. As it progressed, I got more desperate and daring. On one occasion I ate an entire Rueben, only to realize the following day that I lacked the ability to digest it after so long as a veggie. It wasn't pretty.

I realized I didn't belong on the far end of the spectrum, but rather in the middle. And I realized that it was there that most of the answers would be found. I craved steak, though I felt bad for veal and caged hens. If there was a choice between "cruelty" and "cruelty-free," I'd certainly prefer the latter. But I was no longer evangelizing for lettuce or expecting someone to trade their uncle for three sheep. My PETA membership expired. I ordered pizzas with pepperoni on them. And I admitted that I'd been misleading myself a little. The house of cards soon came down.

We live in interesting times. We may have always lived in interesting times, but I wasn't around for most of them so I can't say firsthand. It is a time of massive polarization of opinion and belief, and whether the issue is political, religious, or otherwise, no one is properly served when you stake your claim to the most remote end of the spectrum, so far from any common ground that you can't even find signs pointing to it. Declaring your president is an insidious demon or a faultless angel is as dangerous and unproductive as locking yourself in a Montana cabin and printing your own currency to protest taxation. Extremism is the end of discourse, the refusal to see another side, another opinion, and to ignore that the answer falls somewhere in the middle. Every bombed-out café is testament to the fact that the failure to see beyond black and white is not only ignorant, but unproductive, dangerous, destructive.

Extremism simply wasn't for me, and fortunately it's not for most. Whatever the cause—be it the environment, guns, messiahs, NASCAR, or abortion—trekking over to the far side of any issue and planting your flag there seldom produces worthwhile results. All it does is obligate you to defend your position to save face, no matter how ridiculous it gets. The truth is, you'll find the answers in the middle. The truth is gray. If you want to affect change and influence others, you'll have much better success working at it from near that center where the answers can actually be found, and not from some fringe nether region where there's no room for discourse because there's no one else to talk to.

Undoubtedly I've disappointed Morrissey. I'm neither celibate nor a vegetarian. If it's any consolation, he should know he had me for several years. That might make him happy, though probably not.

Louis Pasteur brought
a microscope to dinner
parties to examine the
food, so if you're a
fellow germ freak maybe
it's time to step up.

Horace Wilcox founded
Hollywood in 1888 and
wanted it to be a model city
of people who did not drink
alcohol. Little did he know, he
was actually founding a city of
people who did not eat food.

11

Deferred Pay

Acting is merely the art of keeping a large
group of people from coughing.

Sir Ralph Richardson

I cannot tell you if the desire to entertain is some kind of genetic defect or simply the end result of a child not getting enough attention during his developing years. I seem to have the itch to entertain, though I can't discern if it's due to my mother's theatrical background or a childhood that left me craving attention. On the one hand, much of my formative years were spent listening to Mom, a former Miss America contender, sing selections from *My Fair Lady*. But at the same time, I had no friends. So it's hard to say. Perhaps it's both a nature and a nurture thing.

Or maybe not. I have experienced in you a pattern of behavior suggesting that you already enjoy performing for a crowd. You seem willing to do anything for a laugh, and any response from the audience—be they bums, friends, or Vietnamese nail-salon employees—virtually guarantees you'll put on even more of a show. This suggests that the desire to entertain might be genetic, as I've not yet had the chance to neglect you.

Regardless of the cause or causes behind wanting to entertain others, it goes without saying that there is a chance you might at some point choose to address those desires by pursuing acting. Perhaps as a hobby, perhaps as a full-fledged career. One day you'll simply don a wig and glasses and pretend you're a lisping bishop.

Fine with me.

Should you decide to pursue acting, I really have no choice but to give you my blessing. It would be an act of hypocrisy for me to say no, especially if your desire comes naturally. I would, however, recommend you don't try to follow in my footsteps as an actor of sorts because they tend to meander and stumble around, and quite frankly I don't know where I've been or exactly how I got there.

Plays, commercials, television, film, and media that hasn't yet been invented—you're free to have at them all. But before you do, take a moment to understand what I've come to understand. Glean a little from my experience. Perhaps my insight will give you an edge on fellow actors, though you technically have an edge on them already by virtue of knowing how to read. Many actors, you see, are thick-like.

For me, as perhaps for you, the desire to perform came early on. One of my most vivid memories from kindergarten—in fact, my only memory from kindergarten—was being told by Mrs. McGonagle that I couldn't perform in the school play because I'd been out sick and missed the one rehearsal. I was utterly devastated by this decision, and when Mrs. McGonagle's daughter later served as my babysitter, I spent much of our time together telling her I hated her mother. It's even possible that I still hate Mrs. McGonagle for her decision. That's how badly I wanted to act, even if the role was a tree.

It took a while, but eventually high school arrived and offered more opportunities for getting onstage. Better opportunities, too, with roles more diverse than "tree" or "reindeer." Roles with lines. Best of all, I was far away from Mrs. McGonagle. There was no way she could stifle the dream.

High-school theater offered welcome respite from being an awkward, shy loser. Thanks to acting I could be an awkward, shy loser pretending to be a lawyer in *Whose Life Is It, Anyway?* or an awkward, shy loser pretending to be a Frenchman in *The Misanthrope*, or an awkward, shy loser pretending to be a persecuted Jew in *Fiddler on the Roof* before dashing offstage to change costumes and become an awkward, shy loser playing a persecuting Cossack. The theater program was short on performers because acting was considered gay at my sports-oriented nightmare school.

I've acted for commercials in radio and television and in short films and really bad corporate videos. I've had the pleasure of working with people I've admired, and some I didn't. I've acted in plays that were good and plays that were not good. I dressed as a Catholic priest and said "Mrs." on *All My Children.* Just "Mrs." And nothing else. And I spent over a decade onstage, improvising in the days before improvisation was trendy. The days when you would say you were doing improv and people would say, "What's that?" and you would explain it to them and they'd say, "So you're doing stand-up?" and you'd say no no no, it's not stand-up, and you'd explain it again and again and they still wouldn't quite get it. "Oh, okay, like stand-up," they'd say. And you'd sigh.

When acting is good, it's real good, and when it's bad, it can make you wish you were dead. The great moments are burned in my memory—the glory of exhilarated audiences, the hearty laughter, the thunderous applause of people who really thought you were swell. But the bad moments stay with you, as well: the painful silence of unamused crowds not enjoying the comedy that wasn't, the lines forgotten in front of a live audience. Understanding what the director wanted ten minutes after the cameras stopped rolling. And the terror of finding yourself alone before a hushed audience, only to realize the other actor in your scene is downstairs chatting with the makeup girl.

I'm not quite sure what we get from acting, why we place ourselves in these predicaments. But we do. Over and over, time and again. We're like adrenaline junkies, but instead of diving from a plane, we play it safer—dressing like a duplicitous Roman or making sweet, fake love to a girl we're really not attracted to.

Acting allows us to cross-dress without being labeled—something an FBI director could never do. It allows us to kiss other people yet not risk commitment, or our marriages. We can pretend to be Renaissance bankers, the King of

England, or a queen in Greenwich Village. We can play characters who are strong, intelligent, and self-confident when, in fact, we're dumb, insecure wimps.

So, yes, should you desire to pursue acting, I will certainly support you. Morally, anyway. Financially you'll be on your own. Making money long-term in acting is like shooting fish in a barrel that has no fish in it. With a shotgun that's actually a banana.

Before you make any decision to pursue acting in part or in whole, you must be properly equipped. Just as with camping or taxes, it's good to be prepared. I can offer you valuable insight on what you'll be dealing with. The only time you don't want valuable insight on what you'll be dealing with is when you're eating a hot dog.

So let's get started.

The good news about acting is the bad news about acting: there is no barrier to entry. Such is the trouble with artistic careers. If I were to declare right now that I was a lawyer, eyebrows would be raised. Someone would ask where I went to law school, and I would tell them it comes to me naturally. Someone else would ask when I passed the bar, and I would tell them I didn't take the bar, but my friends said I could totally pass it. If they asked me what law I practiced, I wouldn't have an answer for that, either. Though I wouldn't be a trial lawyer because everyone seems to hate trial lawyers. In short order people would call my announcement preposterous. "You're not a lawyer," they'd sneer. And they'd be right. The fact of the matter is, you cannot simply declare yourself to be a member of the legal profession on a whim. Ditto mechanic. Chef. Ballplayer. Doctor or pharmacist. Ask them.

But acting is different. Before you even finish this paragraph, you can decide you are an actor. You can put "actor" on your business cards and start your "career" immediately. I put career in quotes because I've always believed you cannot technically call yourself something until someone cuts you a check for it.

Regardless, call yourself an actor and people will instantly accept you as one whether you came from the Royal Academy of Dramatic Art or took a Greyhound bus to L.A. Therefore, even though Maggie's sole income is from working as a barista, should Maggie be killed in a botched robbery, the headlines will read, "ACTRESS SLAIN IN BOTCHED ROBBERY," as long as she had a dream, and a headshot in her purse.

The job title is there for the taking, for any and all. There is no entrance exam. No residency. No forms to fill out. And training is optional. Whether you spent four years at Tisch, four weeks with a monologue coach, or paid $30 to spend four minutes in front of an assistant-assistant casting director, you're an actor. Talented or not, attractive or not, actor or not. For that very reason it is a profession that draws many of the same people for whom warning labels were invented. Labels like, "Don't iron this plastic shower curtain," "Do not use barbecue indoors," and "Careful, coffee is hot."

This preponderance of dunces might serve to explain

why so many in the acting profession are willing to fight tooth and nail for the opportunity to work *for free*. In fact, an actor often finds himself in a career with cutthroat competition for no compensation. I can't think of too many lines of work in which so many people are so willing to devote immeasurable time and energy to something that does not pay and likely will not be watched, enjoyed, or remembered. If I were to ask a surgeon, farmer, or stockbroker to do what they do for free—for hours on end—I'd likely get the finger. But if I announce I'm casting an experimental play called *Der Poopenhaus* that I wrote last night on a cocktail napkin, a play that rehearses for eight weeks and runs one night in my uncle's living room in Yonkers, I will have three hundred headshots and résumés by the end of the week—every single one of them from an actor who dearly wants to be part of my project for not a single penny.

I, too, have devoted countless hours rehearsing for free so that I might get the chance to perform for free to an audience consisting primarily of the director's extended family. I've spent weekends memorizing dialogue so that I might ace the audition for plays and films written by dolts and directed by nincompoops. I've donated hours and hours of my time reading screenplays for ingrates and putting myself at the mercy of individuals ranging from shady to inspirational. Most offered absolutely no return on my investment, and I knew that going in. But in acting, much of what you do is done in the hopes that something better might come of it. That a worthwhile acquaintance might be made. That the play you're putting on—as bad as it may be—might be seen by the right person at the right time and lead to other, better things. More often than not it won't, but you do it—again and again—just in case. You're chasing the dream.

And for those reasons—the hopes-and-dreams thing, the working-for-free thing—there is an abundance of unhappy people in the profession. I've met my share of despondent sorts, from young to old, who've had their dreams dismantled piece by piece. They've suffered, their friendships and marriages have suffered, their lives have suffered as a whole—all for the pursuit of the dream. Some can be blamed personally for their failures; they never should have had the dream in the first place. They're talent-deficient, don't play well with others, or lack the little qualities that make the difference between someone who makes it and someone who does not. For others it's through no fault of their own: bad luck, wrong place, wrong time. The big break that wound up on the cutting-room floor. The pilot that never aired. The role they couldn't take because other things—children, illness, gigs that pay—got in the way. Some of these people are simply sad, but others are quite bitter—scowling when a friend finds success, complaining about the system, and determined to unmask the conspiracy that kept them from their rightful place among the stars.

Years ago, while I sat waiting to play "Man Eating Lettuce" for an episode of *Sex and the City*, every actor not lucky enough to have a trailer to hide in was forced to listen to one man bellyache about how the system let him down. It was the fault of the agents and the casting directors. The managers and decision makers. Everyone was to blame for the fact that he'd had zero success in his forty-some years and was spending the bulk of his day preparing to be another "Man Eating Lettuce." So upset was he with everything and everyone that he was blind to the real reason behind his failure: He was a loud, unbearable dunce. After twelve hours with this man, there was not a person on set who didn't want him to die. Believe me, you'd rather eat boiled trailer-park toenails than spend three minutes with a disgruntled thespian.

And the sad ones aren't much better. At a commercial audition I watched a depressing exchange between two men both old enough to be my dad. Things have been slow in the commercial industry for quite a while, with no real sense that they'll be back to normal soon, if ever. The industry has changed, and along with it the incomes of many actors who'd grown quite comfortable with their line of work.

"How've you been doing?" the old man asked his acquaintance. "Little off, isn't it?"

The other mope shook his head. "I don't have a Plan B," he lamented. "I never thought I'd need a Plan B."

So, should you decide to pursue acting as a full-time career, keep that in the back of your mind. Fortunes change, and if they do, make sure you're not the grandpa without a plan, or even worse, the insufferable schmuck who thinks Hollywood betrayed him and made him poor.

Which reminds me: Don't go into acting for the money. It pays less than a eunuch at a bordello. The odds of you getting wealthy in acting are slim in a field that tends not to pay you. The majority of the 120,000 Screen Actors Guild members make less than $5,000 a year acting. When an actor gloats about landing a lucrative contract, divide that by the number of years he's pounded the pavement fruitlessly. Odds are, he'd have made more money harvesting discarded soda cans.

I like to regale people with the story of how I made $32,000 for ten minutes of work. And it's true. I stepped into a studio, said something like, "That's it, throw the ball, Jimmy," and made more money than many folks make in a year of eight-hour days. Sounds great, unless you take into account the hundreds and hundreds of auditions I've dragged myself to over the years to no avail. Except for a talented few, acting is not a financially sound occupation. When you hear about it being rewarding, they're not talking about the kind of reward you can buy goods or services with. Do it for love, not money.

And never do it for fame.

Those who seek celebrity to cure their insecurities, tortured souls, and defective personalities are a tiresome bunch. Unfortunately they're a big bunch, often found pacing outside the velvet ropes of Los Angeles, pouting and posing, sucking up to and on anyone who can further their desperate agenda no matter how repulsive, noxious, and despicable that person might be. Beware of the pathetic dreamers, the models-turned-actresses and those individuals who labored to develop a persona completely untouched by talent.

Fame should be a by-product of being an able performer. Philip Seymour Hoffman comes to mind. To take up acting because you want to be a star will disappoint you. It's like studying gynecology because you want to meet women.

It should go without saying that a person should pursue acting only because it's something he truly wants to do, yet all too often it's merely the default pursuit of the clueless, the career equivalent of majoring in history. Casting offices are cluttered with men and women who don't quite know what their motivation is. Make sure you know why you're there, and make sure you're up to the task of pounding the pavement with headshots and résumés, throwing yourself at the mercy of audition tribunals, and suffering rejection after rejection. It's grueling, heartbreaking, often unrewarding work, but if you know it's really what you want, you've managed to clear the first hurdle.

Then, we only have to hope you can act.

Women who read romance
novels reportedly make
love 74 percent more
often than women who
do not read them. Possibly
because they have
low standards.

12

On Knots

Marriage is the alliance of two people, one of whom never
remembers birthdays and the other never forgets them.

Ogden Nash

Although the prospect may seem distant and even absurd,
you may at some time in your life find an individual with
whom you believe you could spend all your remaining days.
Hopefully, she'll feel the same way.

Finding that special someone is not guaranteed. Many
of us meander through life without one for a variety of reasons—because fortune chose to deny us, because we didn't
want to, or because we worked eighty hours a week as investment bankers. Discovering someone we believe is the one
for us comes down primarily to providence, a life event that
cannot be planned or predicted. We can endeavor to stack
the deck in our favor, but fate ultimately plays our hand.

Certainly, you can order a Filipino over the Internet, but
even in cases where you ordered a good Filipino, in the back
of your mind you will always know that your wife came via
the same process as one obtains an iPod or discontinued

comforter. Though no doubt there are success stories from such arrangements, I would have to imagine they are few and far between. One party needing a wife and the other needing to get the hell out of Manila is seldom the recipe for romance and everlasting love.

Many years ago I spent quality time with a computer technician as he repaired the network in my office. True to the spirit of computer technicians, he was awkward and slovenly. He was heavy, and so was his heart. Even though I didn't ask him why he was glum, he proceeded to let me know his wife was leaving him. As I continued not to pry and he continued to offer up more information, I learned about his misfortune. His wife came from Russia—a country known for producing beautiful women with a desire to not be there. Women eager to head West and indulge their terrible taste in clothing. Gold pants. Fur vests. Counterfeit Chanel sunglasses adorned with rhinestones.

The computer technician's wife was, fittingly, an online acquisition, like bulk candy or a book from Amazon, and he met her in person only after she stepped off the plane to marry him. He seethed with anger at what he felt was her betrayal, but I assume it came as a surprise to no one else that the receipt of her Green Card coincided with her request for a divorce. He tried to find love and commitment the easy way, but in doing so ultimately got himself taken for a ride.

Finding that special someone just happens, and most often takes us completely by surprise. It's someone we know at the office, or sat next to on a flight to Boise. Someone we grew up with but hadn't seen in twenty years. Someone we met at an AA meeting, and went out for drinks with. For me, it was a Polish girl in an Irish bar in Paris while a brooding Iranian contemplated the best way to separate us. Fortunately for you, me, and, I like to think, your mother, the Iranian's efforts failed. Certainly it helped that he was older and had a beard you could hide garden tools in—and would ultimately have wanted to drag her back to Persia and make her wear a comforter when she went outside.

That chance encounter between me and a woman who initially told me she didn't like Americans started a chain of life-altering events. I certainly didn't set out to get married that night, nor would I have ever imagined it would happen that way. I was taken completely off guard, like a tourist surrounded by shrieking Gypsy children.

We are lucky today in that modern technology allows us to cast a wider net to find people we can date and sleep with. Ironically, the more people we can date and sleep with, the better the odds we'll eventually put an end to our need to find people to date and sleep with.

We are also lucky because when it comes to finding a mate, we actually have a say in the matter these days. It wasn't that long ago that marriage was strictly a business arrangement, men and women becoming husband and wife because of extenuating circumstances like diplomatic necessity, noble blood, or a father needing a new ox.

As time went on, men and women were given more say with regard to the men and women they'd trade vows with.

Suitors could woo ladies of their choosing, as long as they stayed within their class, of course. Ladies were empowered, as well, in that they could say no, though they ran the risk of becoming spinsters if they hadn't settled down by sixteen.

Though people were more in control of their own destinies, the lack of decent roads and painless transport meant their choices were often limited to the men and women of the village. You wound up marrying your neighbor's daughter not because she was your ideal mate, but because you didn't feel like fetching a horse.

Today's advancements in transport and communications have changed all that. Never before has it been so easy to woo—not that they call it "woo" anymore. In fact, anyone who uses *woo* will most likely die alone. These days, it is conceivable to date someone towns away, even on opposite coasts or different countries. Within moments of placing an ad on Craigslist, a woman's inbox will be filled with countless pictures of penises—anonymous, overexposed, out-of-focus genitals from all over cyberspace eager to make her acquaintance. Numerous dating websites exist, making it easier than ever for an individual to broadcast his or her personality and availability to the world. "I'm a social drinker," says an alcoholic. "I smoke on occasion," says the man with brown teeth. "My body type is average," says the 180-pound dwarf. And of course, everybody reads Nietzsche. These are halcyon days for those individuals hoping to eventually stumble across that special someone to whom they long to say, "I do."

But why would anyone long to say that?

Why would someone want to invest in an institution with a failure rate that makes the restaurant business look safe? For the very same reason people open restaurants: success brings great reward and makes you the envy of the village.

Marriage has no shortage of detractors, and one of the popular contentions—especially from males in the twenty-something demographic—is that something like monogamy is simply not natural.

We males, they maintain, are meant to spread our seed far and wide. As the argument goes, to limit ourselves to one person is to ignore our genetic predisposition to hump with wild abandon. Sex, that tiny little word that causes so much trouble, is nature's clever way of insuring the species will survive. If you look at our cousin the ape, they'll tell you, you can see that for yourself. Our cousin the ape hates monogamy. However, what they're forgetting is that our cousin the ape also kills his rivals, eats bugs, and throws poo to express himself—three things most of us are thankfully able to refrain from doing.

Though the ape argument is scientific and admirable, it fails to recognize that we humans, though animals, are better animals and on occasion actually able to quell our animalistic impulses. We're able to see a bigger picture, one that separates us from the rest of the kingdom. We know our species is surviving just fine without our help, that killing someone will sit heavy on our conscience and probably land us in jail, that throwing poo is never the answer to our problems, and that monogamy—though seemingly in defiance of Hugh Hefner's entire existence and our genes' desire that we shower the world with semen—is actually quite a nice thing. Sure, there's something wonderful about sharing our bed with many, but there's also something quite wonderful about succumbing to the institution of marriage. When it's done right.

Doing it right demands due diligence prior to investing. And realizing that, like a needy actress, a marriage requires your attention at all times. There will be peaks and valleys. Squirrels will dart into the road, and rather than swerving off into a tree, we must endeavor to continue moving forward, all apologies to the squirrel's next of kin.

A good marriage is about trust and security, and knowing that no matter what, there is one person in the world who will stand by you, defend you, and whose allegiance is unshakable and permanent. It is about being able to call for backup, and not just hearing static. It's the Starsky to our Hutch, the Burns to our Allen, and in some cases the Tweedledee to our Tweedledum.

Whether you take your vows in a church, a temple, along the beach, or in a pagan ceremony surrounded by grown men with lace-up leather boots and meerschaum pipes, the gist of the arrangement is always the same: the man and the woman are in it for the long haul. With today's life expectancy already not too shabby and growing ever-longer, it is, indeed, a long haul. Nevertheless, all too often we contemplate the entire enterprise less than we would a long-term mortgage or video rental. We bind ourselves to another person with appalling shortsightedness and unwarranted optimism. "Let's see what happens" is an attitude best suited for experimenting in the kitchen or starting a weblog. When applied to lifetime betrothal, it's a recipe for disaster. So do your homework.

Deciding to spend your life with another person necessitates foresight and planning. It should not be impulsive or driven solely by passion. It requires stepping away from the intoxication of our emotions and asking ourselves honest questions that we are prepared to think about and answer truthfully. Can I see myself with this person in twenty years? Forty? Will this person raise my children with me the way I want to? What do I love about this person? What bothers me about this person, and is it something that will fade or fester?

There are many other questions to ask, but the importance of the answers depends on the individual doing the asking. Does she have cankles? Will he still be smoking pot when he's fifty? Does it bother me that she's smarter and knows it?

When making this decision, a decision that will affect you for better, for worse, and forever, you must avoid the external pressures applied by those who mean well, because it's you who will ultimately take the leap, and you who will pay the price for a flawed decision. When a thrice-divorced mother urges her son to get married, he should remind her that she's thrice-divorced. Pressure should never be part of the equation. Decisions, like confessions, are not reliable when made under duress.

Plan accordingly. Marry too young, and you run the risk of growing apart and discovering that maturity and experience have sculpted you into different and incompatible people. Wait too long, and you'll find yourself with ingrained habits, unwilling to make compromises in a marriage. Make no mistake: compromise is as important to a marriage as barbeque is to Memphis.

Once you've asked yourself the right questions and answered them to your satisfaction, and determined that this is, in fact, the person for you, forever, you have done your job. Kind of. He or she has to concur, of course. Then, having found that special someone to share your life with, you can embark on your first journey together: the miserable and tumultuous ordeal known as planning the wedding.

It's said that more than ten
thousand marriages a year
hail from romances that began
during coffee breaks. So don't
think of Starbucks as a place
to get a $6 latté; think of it as
a place to meet someone who
shares your total disregard
for money.

Families that have rules are happier and more secure than families that don't. Imagine the rules are like a guardrail next to a pit—and imagine your family is a bunch of nincompoops who need one or they'll fall into it.

13

Meet the Parents

*Psychiatry enables us to correct our faults by
confessing our parents' shortcomings.*

Laurence J. Peter

Parents bear a great responsibility for the outcome of their
children. They pass on their neuroses and tempers, prejudices and manners. If you know someone who is insecure,
charming, obnoxious, or confident, you can often look at
his or her parents and see exactly why that is. Show me
a stripper, and more often than not, I can show you a girl
who had a bad dad, or no dad at all. You see a guy who can't
take criticism, and I see a guy who never got any from his
parents. We pass on good and bad traits to our children,
from chivalry to racism to penny-pinching to inflated self-
worth. Nature lays the foundation for us, but nurture deter-
mines the building materials and construction quality.

That is why, at some point in the course of a normal relationship, it becomes necessary to meet those responsible for
producing and raising your significant other. This is especially true if you believe yourself to be on the marriage track.

Thankfully we've moved beyond the old days of the arranged marriage and the marriage of convenience. Rather than the parents calling the shots, the actual couples get to have a say. You needn't worry about being forced to marry a mustachioed girl just because her dad is a rail baron or the King of Belgium. You get to date, test compatibility, and conduct research. In the investment world, they call it due diligence.

Your relationship is an investment of sorts, but instead of determining the integrity and financial strength of a company you want to get in bed with, you're simply trying to determine the future of you and the person you're in bed with—and if that future includes a gang of unbearable misfits. Never forget that should you marry, you don't just gain a spouse, you gain a spouse and the spouse's immediate family. These are people you'll most likely be spending time visiting, taking trips with, and, in the worst-case scenario, living with. They might call on you for financial assistance or favors; they might hate your beard, religion, or lack thereof; and they might offer you critiques of your parenting abilities, constructive or otherwise. They could very well make your vacations more tiresome than work. Nothing will ruin your favorite holiday more than spending it with people who can ruin your favorite holiday.

Meeting the parents is an important step in any relationship. It's a learning experience full of insight that just might reveal why your significant other eats with her mouth open, loves Christmas, drinks too much, or doesn't drink at all. It's a form of intelligence gathering that will be quite useful in helping you determine where your relationship may be going, or if you should pull your relationship over to the side of the road and ask it to step out of the car a moment.

Meeting the parents doesn't have to be painful. I was always lucky in that mothers and fathers of most of the girls I dated liked me. I owe that to my ability to be polite, carry a conversation, bite my tongue when necessary, and turn on the charm when needed. In some cases I actually liked the parents more than the girl they raised. When I realized it was time for Grace and I to put our stagnant and morale-crushing enterprise to sleep, I knew I was going to miss her laidback mom and the dry, detached sarcasm of her stepdad. Ironically they were the two people primarily responsible for making Grace the commitment-phobic, emotionally guarded man-hater I realized I was completely incompatible with.

Likewise, I knew I'd miss Lynn's parents. Lynn was my high-school love, and by high-school love, I mean she stopped loving me almost as soon as I left for college. After she told me it was over between us, what added to the pain was that I realized I wouldn't see her warm, friendly mom again. Her mother was a teen boyfriend's dream, who once took me aside to tell me she'd left condoms in the bathroom "just in case." Again, ironically, the same lovely woman who left Trojans in the medicine cabinet had raised a classy, secure, and equally lovely daughter who, sadly, wasn't going to help me lose my virginity. That was left to Maggie, who cavalierly harvested my innocence on a frozen car seat and introduced me to the exciting world of the promiscuous, risk-taking female. I never got to meet her parents, but I'll guess her dad wasn't around much.

Sometimes meeting the parents is painful. Or not painful, but alarming. Either way, the initial discomfort is well worth it if it helps foreshadow danger or keeps you from getting too involved with Mrs. Wrong.

I'd spent a lot of time with Annie my junior year of college. She was a little weird, but it was a likable, quirky shade of Ally Sheedy *Breakfast Club* weird, and I'd always preferred weird girls to boring ones. I liked her, and the idea of being apart for a month over December break didn't appeal to me one bit. We had planned for me to visit her home outside Philadelphia for a few days before returning to school together. When she called to back out of the arrangement at the last minute, I wouldn't take no for an answer. Part of me wanted to leave Boston already, and part of me was afraid she might be starting to sour on our relationship. As it turns out, she just didn't want me to realize that her mother was one of the most unstable women in the universe.

The troubles began soon after my arrival. Annie and I had taken a day trip to Philadelphia, taking in a few Colonial sights and a museum. In the late afternoon, Annie called home to check in with her mother using a pay phone, a germ-ridden device now only used by fugitives and the homeless.

What had allegedly happened while we were away was both amazing and wholly improbable, especially since Annie's mother alleged it had been perpetrated by the family's cat.

The cat—we'll call him Puddles—had, according to Annie's mother, opened my medicine kit, which was sitting on the bathroom counter. This is an impressive feat for a cat, any cat—including circus cats and magical cats—as the medicine kit was zippered closed.

If we are to believe Annie's mother's account of things, Puddles the cat took the zipper pull in his mouth and, using his two front paws, was able to stabilize the medicine kit and open it. After doing so, Puddles then allegedly rummaged through the medicine kit, where he discovered a Ziploc bag containing a very small amount of marijuana. I realize the "I'm holding it for someone else" defense is the oldest lie in the book when it comes to drugs and guns, but I should note here that, in fact, it wasn't my marijuana and I *was* holding it for someone else. At school, Annie had asked me to keep it for her until after the holiday break, and I had placed it in my medicine kit. Not much of a pot smoker myself, I'd forgotten about it and inadvertently brought it to her mother's lair. And the domain of Puddles, the world's only zipper-opening, drug-sniffing cat.

According to Annie's mother—who was in a state of absolute hysterics, mind you—Puddles the cat had then taken the incriminating Ziploc bag and its felonious thimbleful of pot and "paraded around the house with it." Annie's mother went on to say that the sight of Puddles marching around the domicile with a wee bag of cannabis shocked her to no end and gave her grounds to execute a full search of my bags and Annie's bedroom. Though the rest of my luggage failed to turn up anything incriminating, the discovery of Annie's birth-control pills triggered no less than a full-scale mental breakdown. We were summoned home immediately and endured one of the most uncomfortably silent car rides home in history, interrupted by a grueling flat tire, just to add misery to misery.

Once back at Annie's family home, her mother retold the story of Puddles the cat's amazing feat—just in case we were having trouble believing it. It was accompanied by an uncomfortable and memorable icy stare—eyes that were the same kind of cold, dead pools of black that Stalin would have looked at me with before having me shot for whatever. I was then asked to remain on the sofa while her mother took Annie upstairs. What started as a loud interrogation soon turned into a very hysterical accusation session.

They stopped building quality homes in the fifties, so the audio traveled with ease through the wafer-thin floors and down to me on the sofa, making me fully privy to the dialogue. Essentially, Annie was a whore for having birth-control pills, and I was a sleazy drug addict—a bad apple leading her daughter astray. She was a slut dating a druggie. A disgrace. Dreams of the white wedding Mom and Dad had apparently hoped for had been shattered. She was a whore.

And a whore. And a whore. And a slut. Even though I was not Annie's first occasion to use birth control, I fully understood why she claimed I was the only knight to have stormed her tower. However, that only made me Enemy Number One in her mother's eyes, which, as I've mentioned, were Stalin's eyes. But crazier.

The father arrived home from work—having been summoned back early, as well. I can imagine him bolting from the office. "I can't stay!" he'd shout as he snatched his briefcase and keys. "Puddles found weed!"

It was our first introduction, and I'd go so far as to say it was unpleasant, what with him having been told I was a drug addict who'd soiled his only daughter. These are not the best conditions under which to meet the parents, especially a father, but we both rose to the occasion. He was polite and cordial, and after the introduction, excused himself. He went upstairs to join his wife in calling his daughter a slutty whore who'd let a drug addict ruin her life.

At some point in the evening, the shelling stopped, the screams subsided, and Stalin and her husband retired to their room. A shaken Annie came down to tell me everything was okay. Everything was okay, but we'd be leaving for college first thing in the morning—a change of plans that was absolutely fine with me.

In the morning we loaded the car and said our goodbyes, which were awkward, as one would imagine. For a mother convinced I was a drug addict who'd led her whore daughter astray, she was quite amiable, but it was the kind of forced amiable I imagine many mafiosi experience prior to getting an ice pick in the temple.

In Stalin's presence the father was quiet, meek even, and it was obvious at that point who wore the pants in the relationship. He said he'd like to have met me under different circumstances, and I concurred, since the circumstances centered around an allegedly talented cat and definitely certifiable mother. I apologized for causing any trouble, and though tempted to offer kudos to Puddles, chose to bite my tongue. I got in the car, at which point Annie was summoned inside for a final *bon voyage* chat.

The chat lasted three hours, which I chose to spend alone inside the car, freezing. It was a pleasant alternative, I figured, to the warm house where Annie was again being verbally abused. Eventually she was released, and we had an uncomfortable but uneventful ride back to college, where we both tried to reassure each other that distance and time would make everything okay. Annie called her parents to let them know she'd arrived safely, and it was then she was told she'd have to quit school and move back home—or be disowned.

I wish I could say the story had a happy ending—that the mother un-crazied herself or the dad grew some testicles and stepped in, but neither happened. Unable to cancel their daughter's final year of school, as it had already been paid for, Mom and Dad simply chose to threaten and verbally assault their child with every phone call. As a result she staggered, shell-shocked and weary, through her senior year while I desperately looked for an exit strategy. Our relationship was effectively dead. Annie needed me for emotional support and nothing else. Traumatized from being called a whore, she'd shut down Happy Valley and no longer had use for the birth-control pills that had triggered Stalin's rage. As much as I didn't want to leave someone in a time of need, it was obvious that there would never not be a time of need. Annie's parents were a kind of creepy-crazy I'd never seen before, and they were playing a dangerous game—running the risk of turning their Ally Sheedy *Breakfast Club* weird child into a Kathy Bates *Misery* weird child.

One thing kept us together: spite. When Stalin called to tell me to leave her daughter alone—with the Dad bravely listening in on another line—I told her the choice lay with her nineteen-year-old daughter. Certainly someone old enough to vote and join the army could handle such a decision. The relationship lingered like a cat with cancer, with me desperately trying to give Annie an out. Neither distancing myself nor egregious infidelity worked. Finally I put it to sleep with a whimper—ironically canceling a post-Christmas rendezvous. Stalin got what she wanted, and I did, too.

This is not to say you can't marry someone with a strange, difficult, or bad family. But you should always know how strange, difficult, or bad they may be. There are myriad sons and daughters of lunatics, drunks, criminals, and dimwits who may be as lovely as any Brady or as well adjusted as the Beaver. My own mother was a great catch despite being the daughter of an absentee drunk and an abusive nurse. Had my father met her parents, I hope he would have come to realize she had overcome those parental obstacles. Fortunately she saved him the trouble by running away from home as soon as she could.

Meeting the parents will ultimately help you understand the person you love even more because it's part of her story. And like all stories, you have to decide which ones you want to read all the way through, and which are best left on the bookshelf.

**Avoid embarrassment!
If you're planning on
asking a father for
permission to marry
his daughter, make
sure he has one.**

Pirates thought having an earring would improve their eyesight. Why? Who knows. That's why they were pirates and not penning plays or creating legislation.

14

Respect Your Elders, Wisely

The older I grow, the more I distrust the familiar
doctrine that age brings wisdom.

H. L. Mencken

In my youth—decades before YouTube, mind you—I commandeered my father's 8mm camera and made numerous grainy films with regrettable lighting and simple plots like *Matchbox Car on Fire* and *Matchbox Car on Fire Rolls Off Wall*. I dabbled in stop-motion animation to create classics like *Brother Scott Gets Crushed by Garage Door* and *Brother David Gets Run Over*. When video cameras first became available to the masses, I begged my father to get one. When he finally relented, I commandeered that, too, producing hour upon hour of video—from *Brother Scott Gets Electrocuted* to *Brother Scott Cooks Brother David's Head*. Two things became apparent: the demise of my younger brothers was a popular theme with me, and I had an obvious interest in entertainment.

When I chose to pursue a degree in film and television, no one who knew me could have been too surprised. Nothing else interested me, and film school seemed the first logical step in chasing the dream of being the next Spielberg—an ambition shared by most of the classmates I found myself with during freshman year.

However talented we may or may not have been, we all had a strong desire to learn about film—or at least to avoid spending the next four years in business school. We openly disparaged the poor souls studying the dark arts of business, accounting, and law—not realizing that the odds were pretty good we'd one day be videotaping their extravagant weddings for a living.

College was a dream come true. I was excited and eager to learn. For once I could study what I wanted to study, which meant geometry was history. I attended my first classes and enthusiastically awaited what my esteemed film professors had to say. I was not at all prepared for them to tell me the Empire State Building was a penis.

But they did.

And when they did, I'm sorry to say I had no more of a response than, "Okay."

I came to understand that the Empire State Building was longer than it was wide, and as such was a phallic object that represented the male's ongoing efforts to subjugate the female. Furthermore, anything else longer than it was wide was also a phallic object. So, I was told, should I make a film and happen to include a shot of a skyscraper, a ruler, or a sequoia, I should know I was being subliminally aggressive—just another naughty male waving his phallus in a poor woman's face.

Though this might seem patently absurd and hard to swallow, I bought into it. I did so because I was there to learn, and those tasked with enlightening me—my elders—were telling us with straight faces that we should view long, narrow things, like licorice sticks, umbrellas, and golf clubs, with contempt. But their phallic obsession, as it turned out, was only a small part of a general fixation on seeing through the facade and finding the "real" meaning in films. Unbeknownst to me until this point, movies were apparently jam-packed with all sorts of political and religious symbolism, subliminal condemnation of this or commendation of that. Under the guidance of my all-knowing professors, I began to analyze films and decode them, eager to unlock their truths. Some came easy—I can see similarities between Darth Vader's Empire and Hitler's Germany, sure. But others were more of a stretch—is the shark in *Jaws* a metaphor for sexual aggression and class struggle?

Finding the "true" meaning of something by uncovering the hidden and unspoken meaning in it was called "deconstruction." Now that I am a little older and a little wiser, I can define *deconstruction* more accurately as looking at a movie and "making things up."

If you ask why I indulged my professors and subscribed to what appears to have been such absurdity, I can tell you that it's because I was raised to subscribe to it. From an early age it had been impressed upon me to show respect to my elders, to defer to them, the presumption being that by virtue of being older, they were wiser. That is why in my childhood, when my mother's chain-smoking, depressed, chronic-alcoholic friend, Agnes, took me aside and asked if I had any problems I wanted to tell her about, I didn't burst into laughter at the hypocrisy of it all, but rather assumed something must have been wrong with me. I held her wisdom in high esteem solely because she was thirty years my senior, completely disregarding the fact that she routinely drove drunk, using both feet.

I learned early on to look up to everyone older than I, from relatives to family friends to appliance repairmen to my teachers. In many cases it was certainly warranted. But it was a blanket trust based only on chronology, and now included people who were telling me the Empire State Building was little more than an oppressive, skyscraping, patriarchal schlong.

Alas, seniority may imply experience and arthritis, but it does not automatically imply genius or wisdom—as evidenced by the grandma who, after nearly eighty years on earth, discovered hot coffee can burn your crotch. The only certainty is that older means older. Someone may have decades on you, but that's only a guarantee that if nature follows its course, they'll be saggier, toothless, and dead before you. By no means does it indicate their time being older than you was well spent.

I regret someone hadn't told me what I'm telling you now, but they never did, and my education continued. My mind was a sponge, and as it turned out, there was plenty to absorb—concepts and outrages I'd never known existed, much less given any thought to. I learned from my professors that Hollywood was corporate and greedy and that taking that route would be "selling out." This was troubling to those of us who happened to be in film school because we actually wanted to work in the film industry. But we soldiered on, nodded our heads, and accepted the wisdom of our elders. We heaped scorn on the business of film and focused on the art of it—even though we all knew deep inside that would doom us to making long-winded, preachy documentaries about overfishing and sweatshops. We comforted ourselves with the knowledge that we would not be part of the Hollywood movie machine—like everyone we admired and hoped to be.

Everything we had previously thought was apparently wrong. In short order we came to understand that men were bad, white men were worse, and old white men were the root of all evil. As a future old white man, I apologize in advance. We formed opinions that by no coincidence were the same exact opinions of our professors. Christopher Columbus was an imperialist menace, not an explorer; General Custer was a genocidal rogue, not a soldier; Fidel Castro a charming revolutionary, not a murderous despot. We agreed wholeheartedly as our elders foamed at the mouth about politics, denounced this, that, and the other thing, and introduced us to a variety of -isms we'd never heard of. They picked out heroes from among us and hailed their work as shining examples of what we should all be doing. One student, the professor's darling, was praised as genius for his film. It was beautifully done—properly exposed and in focus—but it was about a hand opening a cabinet. Another student, who was apparently pressed for time and out of ideas, filmed a porno video as it played in fast-forward. It was a gamble, but it paid off—the professor didn't see a cop-out, but rather a "scathing commentary on the monotony of porn." So eager was I to please my elders, I set out to make a film about oppression and dreams and freedom and death, but only got so far as to film my roommate, Stuart, acting like he was sleeping. It was poorly exposed and out of focus, and Stu couldn't even pretend to be asleep, but no doubt with a little effort I could have found someone who would have called it groundbreaking or visionary. I can even imagine the lecture:

"What Brian was trying to do here was convey, through the imagery of the awkwardly sleeping man, the fact that many of us go through life vaguely uncomfortable and truly unaware of our surroundings. The harsh lighting alludes to the man's inner turmoil—the struggle for his soul between the dark and the light. The soft focus suggests the man is, in fact, going through life in a blur—nothing is clear to him. This film is a poignant reminder for us to seize the moment, to focus on our here and now rather than the future or dwell in the past."

And that's what the elders did. They talked and talked and talked and talked. No idea was too illogical, no statement too nonsensical. Somewhere deep inside us was a little man screaming, "You can't be serious!" and all we did was shush him because the allegedly wiser ones were talking.

When you hear the story of a stranger who comes to Earth, has special powers, brings knowledge and wisdom, changes people, is persecuted, dies, is resurrected, and returns to the heavens, my guess is—religious or not, Christian or not—you think of Jesus. But if you were to listen to our teachers, it was also the subtext of *E.T.: The Extra-Terrestrial*, and they believed it was intentional subliminal Christian indoctrination. We didn't think to wonder why Steven Spielberg would make a Jesus flick, but we accepted it—again, the wisdom of our elders.

Four years of that, and a lot of retrospection after, taught me a valuable lesson. It taught me that sometimes your elders don't know what the hell they're talking about. And not just when it comes to film. It could be anything. Whether they're trying to tell you that the world is flat, or that you should blow yourself up in a bus to get invited to an orgy in paradise—it's okay to ask questions, challenge statements, stand up and say something smells fishy, or is complete and utter BS. Just be polite about it.

I now consider myself an elder—at least to you—and as such, I encourage you to follow my advice: Certainly you should extend a number of courtesies to those who out-age you. Listen to our anecdotes about marriage and career. Indulge us when we lecture you on politics or opine about the sorry state of something or other, how things were different or better back when. Offer up your seat to us, speak a little louder, forgive us our established quirks and odors—but understand that we are fallible people, and you don't necessarily have to accept what we say as the gospel.

Now, as you enter your *Why?* stage, I seem to be the arbiter of everything you know. That's a temporary position, I should hope, and one I try hard to handle responsibly— answering questions to the best of my ability, deferring others for later. Consulting Wikipedia when necessary. Though at some point, I hope you'll be able to accept that I may be wrong on some things, hopefully not often, but if I do my job properly now, you'll one day be prepared to reach your own conclusions, question answers, and realize that sometimes people don't know what they're talking about—even if they beat you out of the womb by thirty years. I much prefer that to blind acceptance of what I, or others, tell you—though if I tell you to take out the trash, I don't expect counterarguments or deliberation.

I'm inclined to trust Buffett on stocks, Greenspan on the economy, and what Hawking thinks about black holes is what I think about black holes. But you're allowed to have doubts, issue challenges, or even disregard what you're hearing from others. You need not sacrifice common sense or ask your inner voice to shut up on their behalf.

I hope you'll believe me when I say that E.T. was actually about an extraterrestrial, as the title implies, and not Jesus. *King Kong* was scaling the Empire State Building and not trying to oppress, or impress, the ladies. And I'm pretty sure a film about a hand opening a cabinet is as unmarketable and dull as three minutes of my roommate fake-sleeping.

Respect your elders, but do so wisely. Don't be afraid to call a spade a spade when it's not a penis.

Intelligent people have more zinc and copper in their hair, so if you want smart friends, look for the ones with the zinciest, copperiest hair.

15

Friends, Indeed

*Life is partly what we make it, and partly what it
is made by the friends we choose.*

Tennessee Williams

Early on in life you'll find friendships are fairly straightforward. You like Emma, Emma likes you, and you both enjoy using finger paints while you sit next to each other. There aren't too many conflicts, no duplicity or ulterior motives, and just as easily as the friendship was born, the friendship can die—with no hard feelings. It's simply the natural rhythm of toddler relationships, and quite understandable, because you're extremely young, self-soiling, and you think elevators are magic.

As you get older, friendships grow slightly more complex. But they're still remarkably fickle and unreliable arrangements, founded and dissolved over such issues as what kind of shoes you have or if you like stickers. Even friendships considered close can end abruptly for petty reasons, often accompanied by scratching or the exchange of mean words. One moment Doug is your friend, the next moment

Doug throws your crayons in the sewer and makes fun of your middle name.

As personalities develop and maturity begins to take, you'll start to cultivate more advanced friendships—the ones that actually might last a lifetime or a large part of it. At this point you begin to acquire your true friends, associates, and people of convenience.

Knowing the difference between the three is important, because *friend* is a word that gets bandied about far too easily, especially in these gregarious United States. It doesn't take much to be labeled as a friend here; you don't have to work too hard at it or exhibit many redeeming qualities. Americans have a default setting for friend—the exact opposite of your mother's native Poland. There, the title of friend is earned—like getting your rank after passing through boot camp. Before someone calls you a friend, you'll find yourself under intense scrutiny, jumping through hoops and enduring tests of your mettle and willpower. If, after all that, a Pole puts his arm around your shoulders and calls you "kolega," he means it. He'll drink with you and watch your back and even let you play his accordion. That's great news, because from what I've seen, every Polish home comes with an accordion. Make a Polish friend, and the ability to make monkey music is only an arm's length away.

What constitutes our family is left entirely up to fate, but when it comes to who we count as friends, we are the gatekeepers. We set the criteria and make the rules that determine who will pass muster and who gets drummed out. And it's no small matter. Next to family, friends are the ones who will influence us the most in our lives. Sometimes even more than family itself. Our friends are capable of saving our lives, driving us off a cliff, or landing us in jail. They can help us get jobs, or help us lose them, introduce us to our future wives, or fondle current ones.

Indeed, *friend* is a word, like *indeed*, which you should use in moderation. People always feel uncomfortable when *boyfriend* or *girlfriend* is used too soon, so there's no reason they shouldn't be equally uncomfortable when *friend* is employed prematurely. These are serious investments we're making, and like a forty-five-year-old woman who suddenly decides she wants kids, we need to be really careful.

The friends we choose shape who we are. Choose the right friends, and you'll have someone willing to lend you a hand at odd hours and on holidays, someone who knows your favorite password, someone who won't abandon you when you're too drunk to realize you're making a very big mistake. Choose the wrong friends, and you could find yourself accused of felonies, smoking crack the night before your bar exam, or wearing knickers at the Renaissance festival and forcing a bad English accent on people.

Don't take friendship lightly. Let it be an honor for you to consider someone a friend, and back up that friendship with everything you can. There is little I wouldn't do for my closest friends, and I'm reasonably certain I can expect the same from them. You can have plenty of associates and people of convenience in your life, but remember there is finite room for true friends.

A true friend is someone with whom you're most comfortable. There's no need to go about posturing or putting on airs because they know your strengths as well as your weaknesses. You can be you. You can trust a true friend to watch your apartment and not steal from it. You can confide in them and make them privy to your biggest secrets—unless they're secrets like, I buried Bill under the back stoop. Secrets like that challenge even the best of true friends, and I'd recommend not stressing valuable relationships by making them accessories to murder.

With true friends there's minimal-to-nil BS. Rather than fabricating excuses, you can tell them flat-out why you don't feel like going out that night, and though they might try to encourage you to change your mind, in the end they understand and accept your lamentable decision. A true friend knows your annoying quirks and how best to manage them. They will answer you honestly when you ask if your butt's too big. They will point things out before letting you leave the house, so you don't find yourself on a bus with bed head, or sans pants. True friendships can survive long distances and lengths of time when neither party is in contact, and when contact is made again, it will seem as if no time has passed. Very importantly, with a true friend you can sit together quietly and not feel the need to break the silence with inane commentary or clicking noises. Often times you'll worry about a true friend more than he does. Like Mark.

Mark, bless his sweet heart, has displayed nothing short of an utter inability to make good career choices for the entire time I've known him. Nearly twenty years into our friendship at this point, and he never fails to amaze me with his penchant for taking the hardest, least desirable, lowest-paying jobs possible for reasons I can never fathom. Better yet, he's uniquely skilled at taking employment that ultimately results in negative income. For example, Mark worked as a courier and made just enough money to pay for the transmission he blew from working as a courier.

Mark is intelligent and terribly funny and seems to have no qualms about working alongside people whom he has absolutely nothing in common with. People who never finished middle school. People whose retirement plan is this: *scratch tickets.* But he's a true friend, and while I disagree with nearly every financial and employment decision he's made in his entire life, I admire him. I have the highest regard for his work ethic. And his friend ethic. He's never let me down. When he says he'll call, he calls. When he tells you he'll be somewhere, he's there. And I can count on him for anything. If I said, "Mark, I really need you to drive 1,100 miles in a muffler-less Yugo for me and staple a banana to a light pole," I know he would ultimately do it if I asked enough.

Mark didn't ask me what I thought before he decided to go into the karaoke business. That's too bad, because as a true friend I'd have said, "Do not go into the karaoke business." When he charged twenty thousand dollars' worth of karaoke equipment and decided days later that he didn't actually want to go into the karaoke business after all, I respected the dedication he had to paying off his pointless, absurd debt. He could have been a sleaze and declared bankruptcy to escape his regrettable purchase, but he's not that kind of guy. His honesty and personal responsibility are two of the qualities he has that made me reserve a permanent space for him in my small collection of true friends. I often dream of owning a large property with a carriage house on it. Mark could live in the carriage house, instead of his mother's house, and we'd all really be happy. It would never tire me to come home and see Mark in the carriage-house window, or bump into him in the driveway as he heads off to his latest job—licking bus tires for ten cents an axle, for example. If I didn't have a family to think about, I'd be inclined to leave everything to Mark in my will. I would like very much for Mark to meet the right lady and to not be doing whatever he's doing for a living right now. I think about these things often. That's a sign he's a true friend.

Many of the things one does with friends, one does with associates, as well. You have dinner with them, gossip, share secrets, and even attend concerts. They can know whom you've dated and bedded, but they might not know which ones broke your heart. They don't necessarily have copies of your house keys, or know all your secrets. If you buried Bill under the back stoop, that's between you and Bill, and not any associate, for sure. If you move away from an associate, there's a good chance you'll trade sporadic phone calls and e-mails, but the relationship will slowly crumble like Soviet-era cement. Associates might stop by unannounced, which can bother you. When they ask if their butt's too big, your answer will be based on your mood and other factors. You might not point out their bed head because you want to get out of the house. Sometimes, when an associate calls, you'll check your caller ID and say, "Meh," or whatever it is you say when you don't really feel like answering the phone.

George was an associate with whom I spent plenty of time—mostly drinking beer. We'd drink beer and sit around, drink beer and go out, drink beer and try to talk to women. We had some success with the latter, though not a lot because George and I often drank too much beer.

George was painting his apartment, and like a good friend I offered to loan him the equipment he'd need to do so. He collected my ladder, pans, professional brushes and buckets—but apparently not drop cloths, because he got paint everywhere. Weeks after George painted his walls intentionally and his floors by accident, I asked for my things back, so that I might use them for a task of my own. My repeated requests to get my painting equipment returned were ignored, forgotten, or brushed aside until finally, weeks later, George told me I could come get them myself. Eventually I did. To my dismay, the brushes had been ruined from sitting in paint since the day they had been used. The buckets and pans were rendered useless, as well. The paint-spattered ladder and a roller were all that survived. From that point onward, it was pretty much a given that George would never advance beyond an associate. One with an inability to clean paintbrushes. Though I haven't seen George in a long time, if I were to run into him, I'd certainly say hi, and we'd probably drink too much beer and reminisce, but I definitely wouldn't loan him my new painting supplies. Not that I walk around with them.

Associates are important parts of the friend spectrum, offering many of the perks of true friendship but without requiring the same kind of commitment. That said, you can't expect them to be eager to help you move, or that they'll invite you to join them every time they have an extra ticket.

When you have an extra ticket and you can't decide whether you want to invite Curtis or go alone—that means Curtis is not an associate. That means Curtis is one of the many people of convenience in your life.

People of convenience are the no-frills airlines of friendship: they're handy, but usually not for the long haul. You might invite people of convenience to your party, or you might not. They can accompany you to a bar or help you connect your router, and they're friendly like the UPS guy, but you see them as often as you see the UPS guy. Often times you prefer your people of convenience to be among other people of convenience, because sometimes people of convenience—when one-on-one—are inconvenient. When you move, people of convenience soon disappear but are often easily replaced.

People of convenience are habitually forgotten. At 2 a.m. you'll look up from your pint of beer and think, *Crap. I told Curtis I was going to call him when I left the house.* Hopefully Curtis has true friends or associates he can rely on and wasn't sitting at home waiting for your call.

When people of convenience invite you to things, you often have to think about it and weigh your options, because when you're dealing with people of convenience, there often are other options. When considering spending time with people of convenience, you often say things like, "I'll call Bruce if Carl can't go out," and, "Nah, I can't take her right now." It's best when people of convenience don't drop by unannounced, because sometimes you're simply not interested in their presence.

It's not impossible for people of convenience to move up the ladder to associates or true friends, but usually there's a reason they were people of convenience in the first place. A good example is the amiable but boring guy who stays sober and doesn't mind driving you home when you've had too much to drink.

While you should be guarded about who your friends are, you should be open to where they come from. Friendship is about chemistry, not circumstance. You'll find friends in a variety of environments and from all walks of life—and you should. Would you want all your friends to be in carpet sales? Of course, you wouldn't. *We're all going out to celebrate the new stain-resistant wool blend—you in?*

Rich people and poor people can be friends, although they should always take the rich guy's car when they go to lunch because no one wants to drive an eight-year-old Kia.

Be they true friends, acquaintances, or people of convenience, the people you surround yourself with will influence you, educate you, and introduce you to opportunities that could change your life forever. Case in point: I am married, and subsequently you were born, solely because my friend Dave suggested I leave town to celebrate my thirty-first birthday. Strange to think, but you might never have existed had he trashed my paintbrushes.

A 2006 study
states that 25% of
Americans have no
close confidants. No
idea who they
told that to.

Most people don't
realize how many
dangerous items are in
their homes, but your
toddler will find them
and bring them to you.

16

How I Am Different

I used to dread getting older because I thought I would
not be able to do all the things I wanted to do, but now
that I am older I find that I don't want to do them.

Nancy Astor

Recently I was at a relative's eightieth birthday party, seated with family of some sort whose names and relationship
to me I was somewhat unsure of. We were eating our din-
ners and chatting when I realized I was talking to someone I think was a cousin about The Wiggles. For those not
in the know, The Wiggles is comprised of four men, each
with their own trademark color (red, blue, yellow, and pur-
ple) and their own signature hobby (music, eating, magic,
and sleeping, respectively). They sing songs with titles like
"Fruit Salad" and lyrics like "gulp, gulp, drink some water."
They make silly gestures and faces when they sing, and they
ham up the acting to early William Shatner levels—back in
the days when he amused us so often by taking himself far
too seriously. When you watch *The Wiggles*, you're inclined
to laugh at them until you come to understand that children

worldwide absolutely adore them to the tune of somewhere around $40 million a year. Then you realize that these four prancing, jiggly men are making more money than you thought humanly possible, and their work requirement? Being goofy. What had started as mockery turns into envy. Possibly hatred. You fantasize that they have deep, dark secrets to offset the seeming unfairness of it all.

As I found myself earnestly talking Wiggles with people who were just short of being strangers to me, I happened to glance over at my wife, sitting quietly next to me. "Look what's happened to us," she said, shaking her head. Immediately I was forced to reflect on the person I was before I became a father and the one I am now, and ask how I am different.

For one, I find myself talking about The Wiggles at dinner. Gone are the days when I could freely engage others in discussions about sex, politics, work, current events, or gossip about the people we liked and disliked. Now, just in my first years of fatherhood, I find myself eating cold lamb, engaged in a debate over whether the retirement of the Yellow Wiggle will affect the group as a whole. This is the kind of topic that would not have entered my mind or mattered to me in the least only a few years ago, yet there I am—well versed in the story, with opinions on it, and able to recall lyrics like "See him dance in his pirate pants." For the record, I think the audience will be fine with the replacement of the Yellow Wiggle because the audience has a three-minute attention span, poops its pants, and can barely form a sentence.

Another thing that has changed in me is my tolerance for things I don't want to do. Back when I didn't want to do things, I tended not to do them. Call it selfishness or simply being able to not do something, I was able to say no to a wide variety of things that didn't interest me or give me pleasure. It was inconceivable to me to spend time with people I didn't want to spend time with. I didn't go to places I wasn't interested in going. I avoided most concerts, and at the few I actually went to, I inevitably found myself having to get drunk.

Parenthood changes that. You're forced to engage in awkward conversations with parents at the playground. "I'm sorry my son won't stop licking your daughter," you say. "That's okay," says the mother. "Where'd you get his hat?" The conversations are more often than not mundane and predictable: chatter about the schools, the behavior of other children, parents and nannies at the playground; discussions of the merits of particular ages, parenting techniques, and other parks in the area. Dialogue like "The Meatpacking District is full of hot chicks" is replaced by "Last night Tyler had diarrhea."

The playdate is another joy—a temporary arranged marriage of two often spectacularly different adults who'd most likely avoid each other on the subway. Instead, one invites the other into his or her home and forces conversation while their children play on the floor—or to add to the uncomfortable factor—in another room. Women form stroller cliques, the posse consisting of very different, incompatible personalities whose only bond is motherhood. Take the children out of the equation, and you'd have a tribe of women who'd no doubt resort to the time-honored tradition of tearing each other apart.

I've never walked so aimlessly this much in my life, especially while carrying a forty-pound extrovert who wants to greet every bum and inspect every manhole cover. I find myself making the rounds of museums I'm not particularly interested in. Forking over admissions fees knowing full well that five minutes into this venture, we'll be headed out the door. "Okay, finished!" is the dreaded phrase I have come to expect moments after buying a ticket, getting on the subway, or sitting down in a restaurant.

I visit stores I don't really want to visit that sell products I have no intention of buying. *Why am I looking at fireplaces?* I'll ask myself. The answer is, my young companion has decided they are interesting. It's the same reason I find myself wandering the aisles of Home Depot, visiting the vitamin store that has a cat, or looking at absurd art in a Chelsea gallery. How many times have I found myself eating ice cream or drinking hot chocolate I had no interest in? The last concert I attended was The Wiggles, and it was the only concert I can recall attending in a sober state.

And then there's poop.

For most of my life I avoided poop. Like most people, I was never really a fan of it. I didn't like it in the bathroom, or the bedroom. I tried not to step on it when on the grass or a sidewalk. I avoided anything that might put me in close proximity to poop. And on the rare occasions I miscalculated and stepped in or accidentally touched it, I would panic and sterilize my hand for days. Yet, when a child enters one's life, one quite suddenly loses his or her aversion to fecal matters. The combination of squirming child, soiled diaper, and half-consciousness all but guarantees that you will, at some point in parenthood, touch poop. When you do, you'll wipe it off, finish your task, and get to washing your hands when you can. When a perfectly targeted stream of pee was projected into my face, I resisted the impulse to drop the infant and instead screamed and handed it to my darling wife. I spat and coughed a lot and gargled for most of *Dateline* NBC, and from then onward endeavored to avoid placing the child in a position where pee could arc into my face, but I realized it wasn't the end of the world. I survived, and here I am today, capable of jamming my finger in my son's nose to remove a crust of snot. Again, these are things that would have been worth weeks full of nightmares not that long ago. Now they are considered part and parcel for this primary occupation of mine.

Fatherhood has tested my patience unlike anything else, pushing me to the brink of insanity and making me wonder if I'm not on some kind of hidden camera show called *Make Him Nuts*. Seventy seconds to press a button on the elevator. "Press three. No, three. Three. Not eight. That's the lobby. Three. No. That's five. Don't touch that. Three, please.

Alarm. That's the alarm. Don't touch that again. Three. Three. No. That's one. Seven. That opens the doors. Press three. Three. Where are you going?"

A parent can issue demand after demand: "Come over here," "Don't touch that," "Pick that up," and expect them all to be ignored like a UN resolution. Everything takes longer, from leaving the house to getting in the car. And when you have an important telephone call to make or an urgent e-mail to send, that's the moment your child will want you to turn on *Tom and Jerry* more than anything else in the world. Or help him find his duck. Or roll the ball at him.

When my friend Sue, mother of three, was trying to explain parenthood to me before I joined the club, she summed it up in six words: *Your life is no longer yours*. The days of going to bed when it suited me and getting up when I wanted to are fond memories. Alas, fatherhood is not a class you can sleep through. It's not an appointment you can reschedule. You can't call in sick or get to it later. Your child is your merciless taskmaster and is not prepared to allow you to sleep off a hangover or spend quality time in the bathroom. Your schedule is ever-changing, and if you didn't know any better, you might just think your day was being managed by Hitler:

> 2:00 a.m.: *Nightmare shrieking followed by a 4:00 a.m. demand for more water. 6:15 a.m.: Child begins day with diarrhea and bronchitis. 8:00 a.m.: Splits head open on the coffee table as you make oatmeal. Prime suspect in disappearance of wedding ring from 9:30 a.m.–noon.*

For all the random chaos that it entails, parenthood does allow for structure. In fact, it's well advised to establish a routine—something particularly foreign to those of us used to simply doing things when the urge hits us. But structure brings comfort in the form of security. I now have a good idea where I'll be at six (dinner), seven (bath), seven thirty (reading a book), and eight (bedtime). What, to the un-childed, might seem as daily drudgery is, in fact, a very clever and helpful way to keep all hell from breaking loose.

Being a father has made time more precious. When you actually do stop and smell the roses, you appreciate them much, much more. Because it means you have a moment. Someone's napping. That moment of respite is more valuable to me now than ever before. And so you learn to maximize your time and appreciate it when you have it. In the days of old, a long international flight was something to dread. I would beg and plead for an upgrade, use miles if I had to—anything to get me out of coach and into a bigger seat with more legroom and a decent meal. Now, put me in seat 75B wedged between two morbidly obese white supremacists, and as long as I can read a book, watch a movie, and maybe drink a glass of lousy wine undisturbed, I'm in heaven. The little pleasures—reading, showering, leaving the house without twenty minutes of preparation—they're all so much more sweeter and enjoyable to a parent.

But perhaps how I am most different is how absolutely overwhelmingly in love I am with you. The incredible satisfaction I feel at witnessing the very moment new concepts are being understood. The joy of seeing tasks being accomplished. Of three being pressed in under seventy seconds. The thrill of hearing new words and watching how a young mind sees and interprets the world I've taken for granted for so long. Would I ever have thought someone could make my day by pointing out the letter W on a sign? There's something glorious in the innocence of a child as he points to a girl's pronounced front teeth and asks earnestly and sweetly, "What happened?"

To announce that you have a headache and hear a darling little voice ask, "Do you want me to push a button and make it better?" Yes, I do. The ability to act as an analgesic might just make you the greatest child in the world.

How I am different. I'm a father, that's the biggest change. I didn't imagine myself a father for a long, long time. For most of my twenties and some of my thirties, I looked upon parents with sympathy and/or disdain. Parents were annoying, worn out, boring. The concept of taking on such a responsibility seemed absurd. As my friends and colleagues gradually got married and started families, I watched them fall to the wayside. My life was a carefree one of liberty and the pursuit of happiness. I was beholden only to myself, and I loved it. My friends with their spouses and children had lives full of strife, stress, worry, and fatigue. Trips canceled, parties they couldn't make, schools they had to save for. As far as I was concerned, their lives were over. I couldn't imagine why someone would want to do that to themselves. I didn't see any reward in it. All I saw was a gigantic roadblock to having an enjoyable life.

But somehow my opinion changed. I got older and wiser, met the right girl, married her, had a baby. Now I'm different. How am I different? I'm not afraid of poop. And I understand that fatherhood—what I once believed to mean the end of my life—was actually just the beginning of a great new chapter of it.

Van Gogh, Kafka,
and Schubert only
achieved fame after
death, so don't worry.
There's still time.

17

Mortality's in the House

I don't want to achieve immortality through my work.
I want to achieve it through not dying.

Woody Allen

Sometime between birth and thirty-five, the concept of mortality seems to creep in and take residence inside the mind. Perhaps it burrows in. And maybe it's squatting rather than taking residence. Regardless, it's there, and like a determined deadbeat tenant, it's very hard to kick out. Impossible, really. Think *Pacific Heights* with an unkillable Michael Keaton.

Mortality is the sense that you could actually die, and that you should probably prevent that from happening for as long as possible. It is why the idea of weaving in and out of traffic at tremendous speeds is far more acceptable at eighteen than it is at forty. Ditto skydiving. Ditto hanging from a fourth-story balcony on a dare. The older you get, the greater the feelings of mortality become, as they are directly related to the value you place on being alive. The value you place on being alive tends to increase with age, unless you are terribly depressed or horrifically unlucky. Even then, ask most folks if they'd like to die right now, and they're pretty much programmed to deliver an emphatic *no*. There's a reason Logan ran.

We often fret about warfare, and wonder why soldiers are sent off to fight and die at such an appallingly young age. But as you get older, you'll eventually understand why they needed fresh-faced eighteen-year-olds to storm the beaches of Normandy. It's not because fresh-faced eighteen-year-olds have all the answers, because I was a fresh-faced eighteen-year-old once and I had answers, but they were dumb answers. It's because fresh-faced eighteen-year-olds are, for the most part, not the least bit troubled by feelings of mortality. How else can one explain getting fifty men to run off a landing craft onto the shores of a heavily defended beach, so they can dodge mines and machine-gun fire and charge a fifty-foot cliff with bunkers on top? At eighteen the idea seems noble, doable. At thirty it's absolutely insane. A landing craft filled with thirtysomethings would have been an awful sight, indeed: screaming, balding, potbellied soldiers crammed into a corner of a landing craft, begging and pleading with the driver to get them the hell out of there. "We could die!" they'd scream. "Turn this thing around!"

Had the bunkers of Omaha Beach been manned entirely by thirty-five-year-old Germans, they'd have been halfway back to Berlin at the first sighting of an Allied ship.

"Screw this," they'd have said. In German, of course.

A war fought with the thirty-plus crowd would hardly be a war at all. In fact, there's an idea there.

Feelings of mortality increase exponentially once the milestone birthdays cease. The last real milestone birthday is twenty-five, after which you can finally rent a car without hassle. *Hooray*. Beyond that fairly insignificant accomplishment, birthdays serve only one purpose. Starting with thirty, they're once-a-decade mile markers to remind you how close you're getting to Dieville.

Acknowledging your mortality sucks. Suddenly, you find yourself watching commercials about retirement. You use words like *nest egg* and *calcium*. Florida doesn't seem so bad. And the 401K, which in your twenties you considered a ridiculous drain from your salary, is in a tie with fiber for the thing you think about most.

The closer you are to birth, the less you think of death, and rightly so. Childhood should be filled with Legos, bike ramps, and saving up for action figures—not fretting over lumps, time, and genetic predispositions to heart disease. That kind of childhood would make for a very strange child, indeed. For most children, death is simply lying on the ground for a few seconds after being pretend-shot by a friend. Or a feigned crash with Matchbox cars. Perhaps a torched doll. For those of us fortunate enough to grow up in a country without famines, warlords, or sectarian violence, coming face-to-face with death in childhood is an extraordinary circumstance. And even then, a child encountering mortality in some form still sees it as distant and inexplicable. In your youth, death is invariably someone else's problem.

But that youth fades and at some point mortality introduces itself, takes a place at the table, and makes slurping noises while it eats so you know it's there. We begin the slow realization that the odds of our immortality are getting increasingly slim by the moment. We appreciate landscapes and autumn foliage. We start looking forward to seeing the doctor. I never would have believed I'd one day celebrate my birthdays by having a complete physical. Few things suggest the clock is ticking better than having to cough while an old man fondles your testicles and treats your prostate like a doorbell.

We accept that we'll probably never do many things we had intended to do in our youth, which sounds fine to us now because a lot of those things were dangerous in retrospect. There's no way I'm going to Yemen. Learning to fly a plane was heady and liberating. But you'd have a harder time getting me into the cockpit now, especially since shortly after flying the plane all by myself, someone else flew the plane all by himself. Underneath a helicopter. I won't trouble you with the fundamentals of aerodynamics, lift, and rotor wash, but suffice to say that flying a plane underneath a helicopter is the last thing you will ever do. Rest in peace, Piper Cherokee N8447Y.

Inevitably we watch as older friends and relatives do what older people do: Get sick. Fall down. Shatter hips. And die. With an alarming increase in frequency, we hear terrifying stories of friends and associates who are facing life-threatening diseases and succumbing to this, that, and the other thing. Scary things, too, like heart attacks and cancers and falling asleep while passing a semi. I actually know a grown man who choked to death on a sandwich. People are no longer dying from dumb things they can avoid—like hanging off a balcony—but things they had no real control over. Part of the confidence of youth is knowing that the odds say time is on your side. As you get older, those odds start to shift, like your hips. At first, they're still gambling odds. But then the odds are no longer on your side. They're shirts; you're skins. Before long, the odds suck, like betting the typewriter will be making a comeback. Those creepy feelings of mortality are what make a cigarette less of an after-dinner pleasure and more of an affront to fate.

You'll know mortality has moved in when throbbing sensations become potential aneurisms and your jaywalking is safer and more calculated. You go from carefree to care a little. Even life's most routine moments offer a chance to reflect and fret. *What if I have a heart attack when I'm carrying my son? How awful would it be if I dropped dead in this bathroom stall? I'd better not wear my penguin underwear, just in case I fall into a coma.*

Mortality doesn't move out. Sometimes it keeps its distance and holes up in another room. Other times it follows you around, poking and prodding, making sure you know it's there. Ultimately, how it affects you is your decision. Though mortality is ominous, it's as powerless as a British monarch. You can choose to ignore it, Evel Knievel, or you can let it occupy your every waking moment, Woody Allen. Most folks fall somewhere in between—acknowledging its presence but not capitulating. Life's too short to worry too much about dying. And if death gets everyone anyway, what's the point?

When you can finally see that closing chapter down the road, long though the road may be, it is a good time to consider any regrets you may have or will want to avoid having. You can avoid having regrets by recognizing potential ones in the making and heading them off at the pass. They often begin with words like *should have* and *wanted to, never did* and *shotgunned*. Address them sooner rather than later, for when the Reaper is headed up your driveway, it's far too late to start contemplating what you should and shouldn't have done.

The regrets we're left with at life's end will put the finishing touches on our story and determine if the narrative we leave behind is a comedy or a tragedy. Or a tragicomedy. Perhaps a dramedy. They can be mundane regrets, like wishing we'd been nicer to Grandma before she fell down the stairs, or more serious regrets, like wishing we hadn't helped Grandma fall down the stairs.

You can eliminate some major regrets with a little common sense: Spending time with the children you created, for example. Not devoting a lot of time and energy to bringing back the typewriter. And, if you start a sentence with "I know I'm going to regret this," my advice is to avoid doing whatever it is you were just about to do.

Minimize other regrets by taking chances on things that you believe can enrich your life and make it more exciting, the things you know you'll regret not doing. Write the screenplay, open the restaurant, learn to play the piano. Even if there is no reward, or the end result is failure, that's a far more tolerable form of regret than knowing you never even tried. I regret not joining the Marine Corps. I also regret telling my mother-in-law I'd be fluent in Polish in three years. As they say—nothing ventured, nothing gained. Though you needn't venture underneath a helicopter, trust me.

Although most of us intend to lead decent, gallant, rewarding lives, many of us, most of us—actually, all of us—will eventually have regrets in some way, shape, or form. Some of them may be redeemable: the cruise we talked about and never took, the bakery we wanted to open but didn't. Others, not so much: ruining our family by getting caught with the secretary, or telling Hitler he should quit painting and pursue politics.

Eventually we all find mortality skulking around our domicile. Though still an unwelcome guest, if it compels us to take action, then we have at least put it to work—used it to motivate us to have a past we can be proud of.

If you can look back on your life with not too many regrets, I can assure you you'll have lived a better life for it. And nothing eases the sting of death more than being able to shed this mortal coil with few complaints. Passing into oblivion with a look of contentment kills the Reaper's buzz every time.

They say you're only as old as you feel, which is true. But if lots of people are telling you not to walk up the stairs alone, maybe you need to reevaluate how you feel.

18

What Old People Can Offer Us

Cherish wisdom as a means of traveling from youth to old
age, for it is more lasting than any other possession.

Bias of Priene

The older I get, and the older people around me get, the
more thought I give to older people. I talk to them more
than I did. I admire them more than I did. I like them more
than I did. I've come a long way from the days when Peg the
Old Lady would yell at us for playing on her lawn, only to yell
at us three minutes later because she forgot she'd yelled at
us three minutes earlier.

If all goes as planned, I, too, will one day be old—
although I like to think that's a while away. When I do get
there, I hope I will be the kind of old person people say is
remarkably sharp for his age, and not the old person whom
people find standing in the shower with sofa cushions. I
also hope, when I'm older, that someone younger will give
some thought to me.

I've come to realize that older people can teach us many
things, some of which are actually worth knowing. They

come with decades of experience in all matters. They've raised families, built businesses, lived through wars, and survived hardships like the Great Depression and the cancellation of *Knot's Landing*.

Old people can amuse us with their anecdotes—when they remember them—as well as with their ingrained prejudices and utterly impregnable political stances. My grandmother Bertha was a die-hard Nixon fanatic until the very end—never once swayed by his political foibles, allegations of anti-Semitism, or the suggestion that he was simply a flat-out jerk. Not even film footage of Richard Nixon saying, "I hate you, Bertha," would have convinced Bertha not to love, cherish, and adore Richard Nixon. And pity anyone who earned her disfavor. Like an elephant Don Rickles, she'd never forget and she'd mock you incessantly. A decade after the charisma-free Michael Dukakis lost the 1988 presidential race, she continued to disparage "Du-Caca" at every opportunity.

With Bertha, old habits died hard. She paid a visit to her son when he worked at Howard Johnson's. She ordered hot water and a plate of lettuce. When they came, she proceeded to dig into her purse and remove a tea bag and some cooked shrimp. She wanted to save money—an admirable leftover from the troubles of the 1930s, but one that embarrassed my father to no end. Yet he, too, learned from her, and if you ever see a man in Stop & Shop claiming he was overcharged eighteen cents for peaches . . . that's my dad.

Bertha was head of the Grammatical Gestapo, never failing to correct you when you ran afoul of the rules. She would put you right under any circumstance:

"Me and David set Scott on fire!" I could scream.

"Excuse me?" she would ask, indignantly.

"Me and David set Scott on fire!" I would repeat.

"Me and David?"

". . . set Scott on fire!"

"Me and David?" she'd repeat, pursing her lips.

By that time, it would have been too late, Scott would be burned to a crisp—but I'd have learned a valuable lesson in grammar, and arson.

It is because of Bertha's unwavering devotion to words and using them properly that I cannot walk thirty feet in New York without spotting some egregious infraction. Typos call out to me, misused apostrophes might as well have a Klaxon, and I've developed a keen ability to detect when something is grammatically off, even if I can't quite explain what it is.

On many occasions Bertha recalled with fondness a colored lady she knew, blissfully unaware that political correctness had years earlier decreed her choice of adjective archaic and tasteless.

No doubt one day in the far future I'll be musing with members of Generation Z, unaware I'm upsetting them to no end because I haven't heard the term *African American* is now offensive to Caribbean people. I'll appall them when

I make derogatory comments about Scientology, not realizing that a religion created in the '50s by a mediocre science-fiction author is now respected and legitimate. They'll marvel at the concept of a blogless era, when the musings and opinions of every illiterate with a modem couldn't be broadcast to the world with a mouse click. I'll explain what a typewriter was and how hanging chads drove America insane, and my heart will warm when the name Paris Hilton draws blank stares.

The greatest asset any old person has is his or her life experience. When you have the opportunity to interact with an old person, you should. Exploit that knowledge, hear their stories, learn by proxy the lessons they learned. Look at every old person as a potential Andy Rooney—someone who can complain, enlighten, and make poignant comments about life's big adventure.

Bob was in Normandy during the first days of the Allied invasion of France. His squad was wiped out when a German shell exploded nearby. Bob lay on the ground in shock, his leg nearly severed. He watched in horror as German soldiers emerged from the hedgerows, picked through the bodies, and contemplated Bob's fate.

They talked and looked at Bob as he lay grievously wounded and bleeding on the ground. He didn't understand what they were saying, but he braced himself for the worst. *Any minute now, they're going to kill me,* Bob thought. But Bob was lucky. They took his watch and his wallet and cigarettes, but they left Bob, albeit for dead. He lived, and long enough to be able to tell me that story in such vivid detail that I felt like I was there myself. I could hear that story a hundred times and not get tired of it. That's one of the many reasons why you should get to know older folks, and not just shush them or put them in homes.

When your mother and I went on our honeymoon, we took a cruise around Scotland. I learned a great deal on that cruise. I learned, for starters, that cruises are very popular with old people. We were among the few young folk on the boat. But it made sense. A cruise ship is a floating hotel that follows you around. No more schlepping. You make quick stops at ports of call so you can say you were there—in one fell swoop ticking off numerous places you wanted to visit before you died. And the hum of the boat's engines can soothe any arthritic with back pain to sleep.

On several occasions during our honeymoon, we shared our dinner table with other couples. Other old couples. We did this on purpose. If we sat with couples our own age, we'd simply be getting drunk and trading stories about other times we got drunk. Older couples have stories to tell and advice to offer. We wanted to learn, and we did.

I learned that I should have gone into insurance because nearly every old, rich person I met on that boat was in the insurance industry and they could afford to regularly go on cruises. We met a lovely couple—two widows in their nineties—who were spending the remainder of their lives together seeing the world. They'd been best friends for longer than I'd been alive, and they were having a wonderful time. Nothing warms my heart like the thought of my wife seeing the world with her best friend after I'm gone. Except the thought of me not being gone and seeing the world with my wife.

We discovered your mother was pregnant while onboard that boat, though unbeknownst to us, this would later become miscarriage number two. During one dinner, as excited parents-to-be, we sought advice from different couples. "If I could go back in time," said one older man, "we'd never have had kids." His wife nodded in agreement. He went on to pour scorn on his own grown children, who according to him lived in poverty somewhere in the American Midwest. Another woman at the table turned beet red with anger at his remark. Not just because his quip seemed a callous thing to say to expecting parents such as we were, but because, she later told me, she was never able to have kids herself— an obvious source of disappointment. She still seethed with anger the following morning when she approached me as I ate breakfast. "I can't believe that son of a bitch said that," she fumed. "Don't listen to him for a minute!"

I learned many lessons from those people. That life is not always fair. That some people don't get what they want, and there was at least one guy in the lucrative insurance business who was a shitty dad.

My grandfather, who by virtue of being my grandfather was old, was a remarkably classy and chivalrous gentleman. He was always dressed to the nines, even for gardening. He had a suit for washing the car. No occasion was too casual to not have on a vest, at the very least. I admired the way he carried himself and treated other people. He would hold the door open for everyone. Addressed people with "sir" and "madam." He stood up when a woman approached the table, and though some women today might complain about outdated patriarchal this or condescending that, it was simply good manners. He passed on his manners to his children and grandchildren, and for the most part we stick with them, standing when women approach the table and leaving those seated with us to wonder what the hell we're doing.

Fortunately none of us picked up his passion for professional wrestling—his Achilles' heel. When watching the fabricated sweaty ballet that is professional wrestling, he became a completely different man. He locked himself alone in the bedroom, removed his shirt and vest, and disengaged entirely from any other humans. Standing in front of the TV, he was absolutely captivated by the sport, reacting to the fake punches and kicks as if he were in actual danger. He ducked to avoid chairs that weren't coming at him. He felt blows to the solar plexus and punched at the TV set as if he were in the ring himself. He got so worked up that he had two heart attacks watching a sport he completely believed to be real. When each show was over, he put on his shirt and vest and returned to us, his out-of-body experience over until the following Sunday.

From this I learned that we all have our vices. And for the most part, that's okay, though if your vices give you heart attacks, you should probably find other ones.

My boy, old people are a valuable, often sadly untapped resource. Make it a point to find them. They're easy to find because they move slowly. Listen to them, even if they're overcompensating for hearing loss, and learn from them what you can, while you can. They'll appreciate the interest, and your life will be richer for it.

Vaseline inventor
Robert Chesebrough
ate one spoonful
of it every day.
Though he lived to
be 96 years old, he
probably died alone.

Divorced women have more trouble starting new relationships than divorced men. That's awesome news for jealous ex-husbands.

19

Nobody Likes an Enemy

Be civil to all; sociable to many; familiar with few; friend to one; enemy to none.

Benjamin Franklin

Unless we live in an unmarked cave, our lives will present us with numerous opportunities to make friends, acquaintances, and enemies. Heed my advice and avoid the latter. While a friend actively roots for you, and an acquaintance may root for you or simply be indifferent, an enemy roots against you—at best disparaging your character; at worst hoping you'll get colitis.

Enemies are roadblocks on the highway of life. Some are trivial—perhaps a shredded tire or mattress on the highway of life. Others are less trivial—like a jackknifed trailer full of chickens on the highway of life. And some are quite serious—like an armed checkpoint with flaming tires and thirteen-year-olds brandishing AK-47s on the highway of life.

For the most part, making enemies takes effort. But no matter how you conduct yourself or what the content of your character, enemies can always be acquired. Ghandi was assassinated; Mother Teresa had no shortage of detractors; and there's a fifty-fifty chance someone will mock Bono.

Knowing how enemies are made can help you not make them, just like knowing how to handle a pistol can keep you from accidentally shooting Barry.

Some enemies are created by accident, through no real fault of your own. Something you do or say may upset someone enough to take the position of "person who doesn't like you." It can be as easy as saying you miss the Spice Girls. Or petty jealousy of your success. Or the unfortunate result of you dating Martha when Luke wanted to date Martha.

Other enemies are created on purpose because of hasty decisions or poorly planned bridge burning. When my boss fired me by leaving a note on my chair, I was furious at what was obviously not a good way to terminate employees. I took my anger to paper, and in an impressively short amount of time wrote a scathing and brutally honest assessment of my boss and my boss's abilities in the realm of bossing. When my ex-boss read said letter, I instantly gained an enemy, albeit one who had to appreciate my knack for gut-wrenching critical evaluation.

Some enemies are simple by-products of something you do that really shouldn't create an enemy. In my regular appearances on the *Glenn Beck* television program on CNN Headline News, I often critique the host, Glenn, as is the job requirement. Although most people realize Glenn and I are not mortal enemies, some do not—like this unfortunate person who e-mailed me. Subject title: *The Worst.*

You know what the worst thing about Glenn's TV show is? YOU!!!! Brain [sic], You prissy girly man!!! It makes perfect sense: A waste of a network like CNN (Communist News Network) giving an honestly good man a TV show and having your pretty boy ass trying to bring him down. He may have faults and wear wierd [sic] outfits, but who the hell are you to judge him?! . . . Glenn Beck is a good man. And you know it. That is why you have to look so hard in order to find mistakes he makes. You're pathetic and make me sick!!
—Chad.

Last, and certainly not least, many enemies are created by lawyers. Lawyers are veritable enemy-making machines. Indeed, their entire line of work thrives on and demands enemies. At $200 an hour, the more billable enemies, the better. And if you think that a lawyer has any incentive to patch things up between enemies at thirty times the minimum wage, you're sadly mistaken. Lawyers can turn best friends into homicidal maniacs. Sow distrust among siblings. And when marriages fail, lawyers appear like demons on the shoulder, whispering little instigations like, *Ask for full custody,* and, *Demand all the Calphalon pots.* Even the most amicable of separations cannot survive the persistent ember stoking of a lawyer.

If you find yourself having acquired an enemy, it behooves you to determine what kind of enemy he or she is.

Shoulder Shruggers are the least worrisome of the enemy class—the political equivalent of a congressional page—they come and go, but you barely notice, and their effect on your life is nil. Angry Chad being a good example, with minimal influence on my thoughts or behavior. On life's highway, nothing more than a forgettable billboard.

Active Haters sneer and denigrate, tell their friends you're an ass, and try to get you uninvited from parties. They can ruin your chances of buying a co-op, and may sometimes even key your car. You may have earned their ill favor for a variety of reasons. Perhaps they took umbrage because you sent an e-mail that lacked emoticons. Your quaint sarcasm subsequently misunderstood, and received with hostility. They may silently seethe at your fur coat, or outwardly display contempt at your presence. For years I had a sneaking suspicion that Marla really did not like me. As it turned out, she was mad I dumped Sharon—something that Sharon had forgiven years earlier.

Avoid at all costs the True Adversary, he who hates you the most. You're in their thoughts and prayers, but their thoughts are bad thoughts, and their prayers are to Beelzebub. Once acquired, a True Adversary is hard to shake and over time can often not be reduced to anything less than an Active Hater. The True Adversary wishes you ill and devotes time and energy to that end. They long for a grave to spit on, and scan the obituaries in the hopes that one day they'll be able to leap up from the sofa and exclaim, "Finally!"

Avoiding enemies of any type is a wise and recommended approach. Though you may not always be successful, you can greatly reduce the odds of their acquisition in the same way not drinking tequila reduces the odds of you punching a horse.

Changing your exposure to people who could become your enemies is one approach. Sometimes that's easily done—not going to an NRA meeting wearing your gun-control hat, for example. Other times it's harder to do. If, for example, you appear on television and critique the show's host, you should expect that some fans of the host may react negatively.

It should come as no surprise that meddling with people's lives can help you acquire enemies by the bushel. Swindling them, making them generally miserable, and preying on their weaknesses is a given. My old ad-agency boss Larry is a perfect example of someone who has dedicated his life to the acquisition and maintenance of True Adversaries—people who, in the event of a building fire, would gladly help Larry get back in.

Larry's callousness and indifference to fellow man knew no depths, a startling contrast since Larry was one of the most shallow individuals you could ever meet. Larry earned the contempt and hatred of his employees and peers alike with such ease it was as if he was making a concerted effort to inspire a workplace rampage. He was a little man with a big ego and an uncanny ability to win new business. But, like a date with a supermodel, the initial charm soon wore off. The personality came out, and the new clients became former clients often in record-setting time. If we were advertising whores, Larry was the madam, and the clients Portuguese sailors. They came, dropped some cash, and left. Larry got richer. We got screwed.

New hires relocated from thousands of miles away, leaving behind jobs, friends, and family. They came from L.A., they came from New York, they came from over the sea. They bought houses, put their children in new schools, and started their jobs. Some lasted months. Others weren't so lucky. When you worked for Stalin, the measure of success was how long you lasted before you got shot. Larry's regime was little different. A year was forever. And like Stalin's regime, cruelty and indifference thrived. As Barb sat behind her desk weeping and placing her belongings in a box, I stood outside her windowless office with my own box, eager to move in.

In playing the role of self-declared advertising genius, Larry would be as impulsive and outrageous as he believed an advertising genius should be. Entire campaigns worked on over nights, weekends, and during holidays would be thrown out the window because Larry suddenly had a "better" idea.

Whether Larry made an enemy of you in minutes, months, or years, it was only a matter of time. It was there I learned there are three certainties in life: death, taxes, and you will hate Larry.

In our Warsaw Ghetto of an agency, Larry had his capos—those who chose to live on borrowed time. They, too, would eventually meet their fate, which, amazingly, was never at the hand of Larry. For a man who created so much unpleasantness, he could stomach none. Terminations were carried out by underlings, with Larry conveniently on vacation or hidden in his office. From there he would phone the sweet and lovable receptionist.

"Is Scott gone yet?" he would ask.

"Not yet," she would say.

"Call me when he's gone."

I knew I was not long for Larry's world, but I had an instinct for survival. Like Premo Levi at Auschwitz, I endured by having a skill, making sure everyone knew I was not just a writer but also the only person who understood how the fledgling computer system actually worked. In my absence, networks would fail. Printers would not print. And Thomas, my mentor, would have no idea how to turn on his computer.

For months Larry promised me a raise. "Next pay cycle," he would say, "I promise." And when the next pay cycle came and my check remained meager and anemic, I would ask Larry again. "Next pay cycle," he would say.

One morning I received my paycheck. And, lo and behold, my long-promised raise had finally happened. I was now making a staggering $21,000 a year. Three hours later, I was called in by a capo and fired.

Larry made a True Adversary of me that day—but over time has become only a distant, unpleasant memory.

Though he is no longer in my malevolent thoughts and prayers, he should probably avoid asking me for help not falling off a mountain.

There are ways to rectify the situation, should the situation entail having made an enemy. Time, no doubt, breaks down the poison and dulls the sting of the past's daggers. As the years go by, old adversaries soften and fade away. Maturity adjusts our priorities, and careers and the overwhelming demands of child-rearing mean we no longer have time to bother telling people why Betsy sucks.

Communication, the age-old and perpetually undervalued remedy to many of life's problems, can change an adversary to a neutral party, or even an ally. Misunderstandings can be cleared up. Icy relations thawed. Emoticons added. And lawyers' dreams of sending their kids to college on your dime can be shattered with these words: "We're going into binding arbitration, instead."

Forgiveness gives you the high ground. A heartfelt, honest apology can often penetrate even the thickest armor. If you can suck it up and be sincere, there's nothing wrong with saying, "I'm sorry." Even Larry, with his decades on the throne as King Awful, could make a significant dent in his backlog of foes with those two simple words.

Life is tough enough of a game—adding extra opponents is not prudent. Be careful on whose toes you tread, accidentally or otherwise. If someone can't help but hate you, it should be his problem, and not yours.

Donald Trump has picked fights with Rosie O'Donnell, Martha Stewart, and Barbara Walters, but his most famous adversary is still Donald Trump.

Eric II, king of Denmark, died in 1137. Though he's known as Eric the Memorable, no one knows why.

20

Live to Be Missed

When good men die their goodness does not perish, but
lives though they are gone. As for the bad, all that was
theirs dies and is buried with them.

Euripides

If life is a party, you should endeavor to be the life of the
party, or even the guy who stands quietly in the corner of the
party, with occasional trips for more cheese cubes and Char-
donnay. Just, please, don't be the guy at the party everyone
hopes will be leaving soon.

Life is an intolerably temporary arrangement, something
you'll come to realize soon enough. We have a certain, seemingly random period of time in which to do things. They can
be great things, mediocre things, or terrible things. Or you
can sit on the sofa, do no things, and let it all pass by. But
there's one thing that occurs to me every time I drive by the
enormous cemetery in Queens or stroll the graveyard in your
mother's tiny Polish village: at some point, everything we do
and don't do while we're here will be naught but a memory.
How we lived will be our legacy, and how well we played
with others our epitaph. Will it be "Fred was a great guy" or

"Fred owed me a hundred grand"? Ultimately that's up to Fred. Whether the memories of you are tainted, cherished, abhorred, or adored is your call. You drive that bus.

My grandmother Bertha was a remarkable woman. She was vibrant and good-humored, and as a result always surrounded by people who loved and cared for her—people who wanted to be around an old lady. Not because of necessity or obligation, but rather love and adoration. She was like a rock star in that respect, but one who had arthritis and a road map of veins on her chronically swollen legs. She was fallible: wholly incapable of eating anything without it winding up on whatever she was wearing. Any outfit she wore was technically a bib. If you were to stitch together all the fabric she'd stained in her lifetime, you'd have enough to cover all the ugly parts of Pittsburgh.

But what I remember most about Bertha, aside from the name and the dribbling, was that she was good. She radiated it. And for as long as I can remember.

Bertha was merciless and unbeatable in checkers. She had a tendency to worry too much, and an overactive imagination that led her to believe doom was everywhere. She once warned me not to go to Ireland because, as she understood it, the place was teeming with bombs.

She was adorably naïve about some things. In my teens I would pay her a visit and be offered wine coolers. She was completely unaware they had alcohol in them. At some point she learned the truth, a day I remember well.

"Where are the wine coolers?" I asked.

"They had alcohol in them, can you believe that?" she replied.

"No," I lied.

Bertha smiled a lot and laughed plenty, presumably because she was happy. Whenever she remembered her late husband, Sam, she'd tear up and recall what a good, thoughtful gentleman he was. She missed him, as you would someone you'd been married to for over half a century. I was always touched by that, and hope that one day, fifty or seventy years from now, your mother will get sad and sentimental about me. She'll take a deep breath, and sigh, and mumble something about how great I was. Everyone in the room will nod in agreement. And then they'll all leave flowers and other offerings at my statue in the garden.

Grandma once shared with me her fundamental philosophy: *It's good to be good.* That was pretty much it. She offered no explanation why it was good to be good. There was no alternate viewpoint. It was just understood—a simple nondenominational ideology. It didn't require any leap of faith. There were no deities involved, no threats of eternal damnation if you weren't good, or good enough. And there were no promises that being good would bring you happiness, help you win the lottery, or land you in some sort of eternal paradise. It was simply good to be good, and that was that. A person either believed it or he didn't, and if he didn't believe it, that meant he thought it's bad to be good or it's good to be bad—both valid reasons to avoid him because he was either dumb or trouble, respectively.

Though Bertha had every right to be angry and bitter for being saddled with a name like Bertha, it didn't phase her. She just did her thing, which was to show up on Sundays with corned beef and coleslaw and potato salad. We'd eat well, then she'd completely destroy us in checkers with no regard for our age difference. We looked forward to her— not just for the food and definitely not for the schooling in checkers, but because she was mighty pleasant to have around, smiling and chuckling and making the room a warmer place. She was good. She wasn't brownnosing for some kind of cosmic points. It was simply how she was. It's what she believed she should be. And it was a belief that paid off in spades because everyone cared for her to the very end. When that end came, everyone knew that they'd lost somebody good, and something valuable. Especially the neighborhood dry cleaner, who had profited greatly at Bertha's inability to not spill soup on herself.

The end came when she was ninety-two, and it came at home—because when you're a good person, people actually don't mind living with and being around you. She had lived with her brother, daughter, and son-in-law for fifty years. In her twilight, as will happen when you're nearing a century old, her health slowly deteriorated. She slept more and more and felt weaker and weaker until one day was the last day. She watched the hard-working home-care nurse leave the room and turning to her daughter said, "Be sure to give her double." Those were her last words. She exited the world in good humor. A cheerful soul to the very end.

We were all very saddened to lose her, and we all miss her a great deal. She was right. It *was* good to be good.

By contrast, when my maternal grandmother died, I didn't know for weeks. Maybe months. One day a letter arrived, sent not by friends or family but by probate court. This was a solely legal procedure to make sure I knew my mother's mother was dead in case I had any claims on her estate. I didn't—I'd never known her. Until that letter came, I hadn't even known for sure what her name was. My mother had run away from her as soon as she could and never looked back. Not even the looming specter of my mother's death was enough to warrant reconciliation.

As a result I never saw a picture of or heard a kind word— any word—about Anne Marie. I'll probably never know who, if anyone, was around her when she died. I just know that none of us were. And that's a shame.

That sad chapter made me realize that no one misses a bad guy, or a bad grandma for that matter. If you want people to care about you during and after your life, you need to endeavor to make them do so. You don't do that by making them miserable, robbing them, or storming into their office and shooting them. You need to be good to them. That's not always easy, sure, but like all things that take effort, there is a reward. In this case, the reward is that people are sorry to hear that you got hit by a truck or were felled by rabies.

Take Mark, for example. Mark is good and always has been. He's always sincere and mighty pleasant and wholly trustworthy. How trustworthy? If I were to kill a leprechaun and ended up with a heavy pot of gold, he would watch it for me while I ran off to rent a van. And when I came back with the van, all the gold would still be there. Every single piece of it. And even if he was running late, he'd help me load the van. And if I asked Mark not to tell anyone I'd killed a leprechaun, he'd agree. But deep down I'd know that he's such a good person, his conscience would eat him alive to keep such a secret. So I'd have to kill Mark, too. That's how good he is.

And Mark keeps on being good, even though it hasn't earned him any cosmic reward points. He works hard for little money alongside people who think prepositions are fancy talk. It's thankless, manual work. Mark has plenty of reasons to not be good, or to be less good, yet he's really good. There's not one person who knows him who's not a fan and a cheerleader. To know Mark is to hope he wins the lottery, finds the right girl, and lives happily ever after. Mark's friends fret about Mark's career and future more than Mark does. That says something about good people. It's good to be good.

That's why I don't park in the handicapped spot because it's more convenient. I don't treat people like dirt, vandalize phone booths, or steal the life savings of the elderly. That doesn't mean I don't get annoyed at people who are too slow on the sidewalk. It doesn't mean I tolerate bad waiters well or that I'm a perfectly thoughtful husband who never makes his wife mad. I'm plenty fallible. But I do know, deep down, that my life is richer and more rewarding because I bought into my grandmother's ideology. I do believe it's good to be good, no strings attached. We only have a short time on this stage. As the curtain comes down on the final act, the last thing I would want to see is the audience frowning at me.

Though I'll probably never be as good as Mark, and lots of other folks, with enough effort I can still earn the right to be remembered as a good husband, friend, father, and human. That way, when my last day comes, you and everyone else left at the party will be able to say, *You know, I'm sorry that guy left*. And no one will have to stretch for a eulogy like, *Brian loved bacon . . . and he was good at darts*.

Dear Son:

I realize that the knowledge and wisdom you may have acquired by reading, or skimming, this book may not be the greatest assembly of knowledge and wisdom in the world—especially when compared to that of Socrates or Wikipedia—but it certainly beats acquiring no knowledge or wisdom. You're at least somewhat better off for it. A little farther ahead in the animal kingdom, which is always helpful. Even a tiny bit matters when you're trying to distance yourself from something that slings feces.

Of course, there's certainly much, much more to learn. Every day presents new experiences—new opportunities to acquire even more knowledge and wisdom. And that's not just for you, but for everyone, myself included. In fact, when I began this book, I was writing to a son. Now I have two sons, both students at Great Big University, whom I hope will someday profit from what little I know.

I will endeavor to help you both as much as I can. Alas, there will be things I am neither privy to nor able to convey, things I simply will not know and things you won't find in books. No book could prepare you for everything anyway. A book like that would take tremendous amounts of time. And colossal amounts of paper. Not to mention—it would be a very large book, the kind that you wouldn't be inclined to purchase because it's just too big to walk around with. Plus, even if it were broken down into tinier, more manageable segments, you'd get annoyed around the ninth edition and say, "Yes, yes, I get it," because really—you want to experience life yourself.

As you should. A life spent not experiencing things is a tragedy. The world is a great big, fascinating place worth checking into. Take advantage of your time at Great Big University and get the best education you can. Get out there and live and learn, because at some point we all graduate for good.

Speaking of which, should you have any further questions or things you'd like me to elaborate on, I'm uncharacteristically optimistic that I'll be here for some time to assist. My untimely demise is, hopefully, hypothetical. I'm not that old and with any luck I'm in good health.

Love,
Dad

Acknowledgments

This book is the end result of a bizarre and interesting chain of events—a lesson in and of itself that life is wholly unpredictable and intrinsically weird.

Like all books, it was dependent on the cooperation, support, and understanding of numerous individuals to ensure that it would actually see the light of day.

It was also dependent on dumb luck. How this book actually came to pass went like this: I overheard a stranger, Amy Keyishian, telling a friend about something hilarious she'd seen on the Internet. It turned out to be *Please Stop Reading Us Magazine*, an open letter I'd written to my wife that Gawker .com, a website I'd never heard of, had picked up. That led me to Gawker's editor, Choire Sicha, who told me to write more—something I'd heard a lot from friends and family and ignored. Even though I didn't know Choire from Adam, I took his words to heart and soon created Banterist, my website of original humor. The desire to continually churn out material resulted in me eventually posting an ad on eBay for my unfortunate leather pants. The ad hit a nerve to the tune of over 3.4 million hits. From that came countless e-mails from the news folks, the agents, the producers, the aspiring writers, the single, the desperate, the crazy, and, very importantly, the many folks who said, "You should write a book."

Fortunately I had a body of work as a freelancer and blogger that suggested I just might be able to do that.

It's nice being approached by agents. I immediately liked Sara Crowe at Harvey Klinger. We worked together on a proposal, which she dutifully shopped to the right folks at the right places. Eventually a deal was made, a contract signed, and I realized I had a book to write.

Other authors told me their horror stories about painful relationships with editors and publishers. Fortunately, I didn't experience that, and I can thank Cynthia DiTiberio at HarperOne for her gentle stealth editing and valuable suggestions that actually improved the book.

Without the cooperation of my superstar wife, Ewa, I would never have finished the book on time, if at all. Her assistance was paramount—allowing me to wander off and write undisturbed while she skillfully parented one, then two, children. Though fatigued and overwhelmed at times, she never complained but merely demanded I finish on deadline so that I could return to assist her in the art of child-rearing—which isn't so much an art as a let's-see-what-happens-when-we-do-this kind of thing.

My superstar wife's mother Janina Tomaszewska helped cook, clean, assist, and child-rear so that I might play author. Her assistance was beyond priceless, and the fact that she lived with us for months and I still love her suggests she's the greatest mother-in-law one could ever hope for.

William Craig, Dave Kiesgen, and David Sack became unlikely babysitters—providing me with additional valuable hours to not be a parent so I could ironically write about being a parent. To them I'm very grateful.

Lila Cecil and Joy Parisi provided Paragraph, the writer's space where much of the book was written. Burton and Gail Sack provided Parents' Empty House, where the rest of it was written and I was free to walk around reading to myself out loud. Without those sanctuaries I'd have lacked the necessary peace and quiet one apparently needs to write a book. It's really hard to focus when there's a child tugging on the doorknob.

Of course, I owe immense thanks to my mother, Susan Lightbown Sack, whose inspiring, comforting letter delivered at the height of my childhood's greatest misery set the stage for the book you're reading now.

She wrote, "I pray that you find something to devote your life to that is meaningful and rewarding—something that brings you joy."

Done.

NEW YORK CITY
August 2007